A War Bride's Memoirs

Also by Roger Brown:

The Truth Seeker's Handbook
Heading Out
Encounters
Insights
33 Years of Dreams

A War Bride's Memoirs

Audrey Brown

Memoirs of Audrey Brown
Covering her first 53 years

London, England, 1920 -
Rancho Bernardo, California, 1973

Edited by Roger Brown

Golden Galaxy Publications

Published by Golden Galaxy Publications
Copyright 2015 Roger Golden Brown
ISBN: 978-0-9743513-3-9

You are free to copy and redistribute the material under the following terms:

Attribution - You must give appropriate credit and indicate if changes were made. You may do so in any reasonable manner, but not in any way that suggests that I endorse you or your use.

ShareAlike - If you change the material in any way, you must distribute your contributions under this same license.

No additional restrictions - You may not apply legal terms that legally restrict others from doing anything this license permits.

Please contact me if you have any questions.

I can be contacted at the following e-mail address:
wordsmith@goldengalaxies.net

Visit my personal website:
https://goldengalaxies.net/

And check out my world affairs oriented website:
https://goldengalaxies.net/Quasar/

This book is available for sale at:
http://books2read.com/rogergoldenbrown

See all of my books at my Author Page:
http://books2read.com/rogergoldenbrown

Editor's Note: The editing process consisted of me, Audrey's son, converting the old typewriter manuscript (replete with weak and faded letters) into a computer text document and cleaning up some typos. The content was not changed in any way, except that beyond the occasional translation of a British English word that my mother added in parenthesis, I added a few more. My mom never made a table of contents but I put one together as a reference so the reader can better navigate the book. And I have included some photos at the end of the book.

Table of Contents

London, 1920...1
Mary Datchelor Girls' School, 1931..................................42
Spectre of War, 1938..68
Bath, 1939..73
Jake Brown, 1943..93
Back to London, 1944...102
War Brides Travel to America, 1946...............................107
America..120
Newlyweds Reunite, Longview, Washington..................135
Seattle..144
Lake Forest Park, 1956...154
Rancho Bernardo, California, 1973................................161
Epilogue...165
About the Author..166
Photos..167
Books by Roger Brown...174

London, 1920

Where do I begin? At the beginning I suppose. When I was born my mother haemorrhaged badly and the doctor, called in at the eleventh hour by the midwife attending her at home, decided that he could not save us both and my mother was given priority while I was put aside to expire peacefully and with as little trouble as possible. My mother lived to 94 and with an inherent cussedness I began to scream lustily and also emerged from the ordeal in good shape.

I was born in London to a middle class family. My father had been in Germany in the army of occupation until the end of 1919 and when he returned home and to civilian life he found that the land "fit for heroes to live in" had for a start no homes for them to live in. Not long after I was born we moved up a peg and from sharing a very small house we moved into the top half of a larger house with a small garden that my five year old brother could use - if the house owner was in a good frame of mind that day.

Dad worked In some mysterious place called "THE OFFICE" and as any matters pertaining to the adults were never discussed before the children it was years before I had even an inkling of what THE OFFICE might be and not until I was almost ready to embark on my own career did I discover exactly what Dad did for a living. He was employed by a very old established firm of importers and exporters and by the time I was in my teens he was export shipping manager and the financial hardships of those long years after the war trying to establish himself had eased.

Mum was a housewife, not in the slightly derogatory sense that the word is used today but in the full, wonderful meaning of the word. To my father she was lover, friend and helper in every way. To us children she was a loving teacher and confidant, a kindly disciplinarian and a tough fighter to help us achieve our aspirations. For all of us she was cook, laundress, housekeeper, organiser and economist. Not until after Dad retired did she ever know what salary he received but each pay day she thanked him for the "housekeeping money" he gave her, she made it go a long way and we never wanted for any essentials. And even in the toughest times there was always a little bit left over for a treat here and there that added joy to our life. She never had a cheque book until after Dad died, never had a credit card in her life but she knew how to get full value for every penny and in doing so kept us happy and healthy.

I have few actual memories of these early years but one of the recollections I do have is sitting in the window facing the street and counting cyclists coming back from a day trip into the country. Back then you did not have to go very far from suburban London to be in stretches of woodland and open country and every Sunday the streets were full of people going off on their bikes to picnic at some beauty spot. Few people had cars and a bike was the normal mode of transport. In the spring the cyclists would pick great bunches of bluebells that grew wild in the woods and would carry them home strapped on the luggage racks of their bikes. Mum and Dad had many a peaceful Sunday afternoon by the simple expedient of sitting me up by the window with a paper and pencil to count the cyclists, one count for a bike and two counts if it was carrying bluebells. I was paid the

London, 1920

magnificent sum of a ha'penny (1/2d.) for every hundred I counted. No wonder I could count long before I went to school!

At one time either my brother or I told Mum and Dad that there was a hymn we sang in Sunday school that was all about the Sunday cycles. It took a lot of head scratching and confusion before the hymn was finally identified by Dad as being "Stern Disciples"! This reminded Mum of a similar occasion when Doug was much smaller and before I had arrived on the scene. Dad was overseas in France with the army during the war and Doug was given a new teddy bear. He told Mum he was going to name it "Gladly". Mum thought it was rather an odd name but Doug said that it was because of the song in Sunday school and after all the teddy was just a little bit cross eyed. This statement was not very enlightening but when Dad came home on leave he settled the mystery by remembering a song he had sung in church as a boy, "Gladly my cross I bear".

In later years telling this story Mum said that this particular leave of Dad's was one to remember in many ways. There was a bad zeppelin raid the night before Dad was due home and Mum and her sister with whom she shared a house at that time with both the husbands gone decided to dash off down the street to their mother's house for shelter and company. They got the children, including her sister's newborn baby, up and dressed but by the time they got everything organised the raid was over. They decided that as long as they were all up they might as well go anyway as they were sure their mother would want to know that they were safe. I never heard what my grandmother thought of this 2am visit!

The house had an old coal burning stove that the two women were always complaining about saying that it couldn't even get hot enough to cook a milk pudding (usually by this meaning a rice dessert). When Dad got home his army greatcoat was full of lice from the trenches in spite of the certificate that I still have that says he was free from vermin and fit to travel! The men left the trenches and went directly to the transport trains and boats bringing with them all their equipment and uniform items. As he and Mum were going out for the evening Dad decided to pop his greatcoat in the oven so that the heat, even though limited, would kill the lice and as the oven was no longer used for cooking food anyway. Naturally on that night the oven decided it had taken enough abuse and decided to heat up and when Mum and Dad got back the coat was a mass of charcoal - sixty years later Dad still laughed over their reaction when they saw what had happened. Mum was very upset and afraid that Dad would be court-martialled for destroying army property and his amusement at the whole affair didn't help a bit. Finally Dad pointed out that as it was summer he did not need the coat while on leave, and when he got back he would be going straight to the trenches to relieve others going on leave and he would have no problem at all helping himself to another coat from the first body he saw. This reminder of the appalling slaughter did not exactly bring Mum peace of mind but at least she no longer worried about the coat.

Although, as I have said, the house we lived in when I was very small was owned by someone else and we only had the top floor we did for a while have a puppy and a kitten. Dad would take the puppy for walks on a lead and all he had to do was to rattle the lead and the pup went crazy with

London, 1920

excitement running around in happy anticipation. The cat watched this performance a few times and decided that she would like to join in the fun so from time to time she would jump up on the banisters, reach for the lead that hung nearby on the wall and rattle it. The poor dog would come skidding across the linoleum floor, eyes bright and tail wagging only to find it was a false alarm while the cat sat there, looked at the dog and smirked. This game came to an abrupt end one day. When Mum cleaned the floors she would first clean the rugs and then hang them over the banisters out of the way until the floor was done. One day when the cat jumped up to tease the dog there was a carpet there and not being quite centred the moment the cat hit it, it flipped over and with the cat rolled inside it fell to the floor beneath. The cat was not at all hurt but it never again jumped up to tease the dog.

There is a sad ending to the story of this pup. My brother, Doug, took him out one day and he suddenly pulled the lead out of Doug's hand, dashed into the traffic and was hit by a car and killed instantly. I have only a vague remembrance of being in the house when Doug came in crying followed by a neighbour to tell Mum what had happened. The neighbour took care of me while Mum went back with Doug but there was nothing that could be done. There were some men working on the road and one of them brought a sack and picked up the pup and told Doug they would bury him nicely in a hole they were digging by the roadside. After that we did not have a dog for several years.

It was on that same rather dangerous corner of the road that a couple of years later on my way home from school I was knocked over by a cyclist as I had dashed across the road without "looking both ways" as had been drummed into me as soon as I could walk. I was not hurt, just a bruise, and as it was obviously my fault I never breathed a word to anyone. In fact for a few days I lived in fear of the cyclist coming to the house and lodging a complaint against me.

The house we lived in and all the houses around us had been built many years previously on land that had originally belonged to the owners of what I suppose could have been called a small manor house. The "manor" had long since gone although there was still a large house standing in extensive grounds surrounded by a high brick wall. At the very end of our street where it joined the main road there still remained the cottage, the house that had formerly been the gate-man's home at the entrance to the estate. My mother knew the older woman who lived in the cottage and once in a while she was asked in for a cup of tea on her way back from the shops. I was entranced with this old house. It was very small but had a winding staircase going up to an attic and the windows were all leaded with panes of glass in diamond shapes just like those shown in books of fairy stories. Mrs King, the owner - or more probably the tenant - of the house always gave me a biscuit and let me wander up to the attic and watch out of the windows.

She is the only neighbour I can truly remember, probably because of her being associated with this "fairy" house. In later years I got to know other neighbours by name from hearing my parents talk about them. One, apparently, was always trying to find out Mum's age by asking Doug oblique questions such as how old was Mum when the war started etc. Mum finally told Doug to tell Mrs Penny that she was as old as her tongue and a little bit older than her teeth. Not a bad answer but I doubt that Doug passed it on. I found out

London, 1920

later that my parents referred to this neighbour, Mrs Penny, as "Mrs Coin-of-the-realm" in front of us children so that we would not know who they were talking about. Apparently she was not the most popular person with my parents.

When I was very small Mum had an accident in this house that could have had serious consequences. Mum used to put her washing out to dry on a line in the back garden. When she wanted to bring in the dry things she would take a large wicker basket with her and bring the filled basket up the stairs to our part of the house. At the top of the stairs was a gate to keep me in and to unfasten it to let herself in Mum would put the basket on the stairs behind her. One day just as Mum had done this Doug called from down below. Without thinking Mum turned around and moved towards him, fell over the basket and crashed down the whole flight of stairs.

Of course in those days no one ever went to a doctor unless they were dying so Mum put up with the pain and black eye for several days. Finally Dad said that perhaps she should "pop in and see old Mr X" who kept the chemist shop on the corner. The chemist gave her some aspirin and said she should consider going to the doctor if the pain persisted. When she eventually went she found that she had fractured her cheekbone but that it had begun to knit very nicely and there was no treatment necessary. This was very fortunate for if she had been taped up in the rather primitive methods of the twenties she would probably have been disfigured and had continuing problems.

I started kindergarten soon after I was four. It was a full day of schooling although we did have a little rest period in the afternoon. Thanks to the cyclists I knew how to count and thanks to Mum and my big brother I also knew my alphabet and could read easy words. Of course we were big on phonetics and reading was stressed at an early age. There is a story told of me at this time, nothing that I remember and nothing to do with book learning. I had just turned five and was able to walk to school by myself, it was only about half a mile and I walked with other children. Apparently on this day, shortly before "going home time" tragedy struck in the shape of broken elastic in my knickers (panties), which promptly fell to my ankles. I could not walk home clutching them around my waist, to take them off was unthinkable and to tell the teacher was just as bad so I sat huddled in a corner of the shed (a covered portion of the playground) and crying miserably. My mother, meanwhile, was beginning to get a bit worried as I did not show up at home at my usual time. She continued getting tea ready with one worried eye on the road outside the window. A knock on the door and there stood a boy, another kindergarten child. "Mrs Avis, Audrey can't come home. Her drawers have fallen down!" Poor Mum, she thanked the boy, got her coat and hat and gloves on and set out for the school with a replace pair of "drawers" in her handbag. My brother thought it was all very funny until he was sharply reminded that gentlemen did not laugh at such things. In fact gentlemen were not supposed to know that such undergarments existed!

When I was about six we moved to a house farther out from the city in an area of Kent called Grove Park. The house we rented was new and rented not from an individual but from the local council. I suppose today it would be called "low income housing" but in the twenties every one was low income trying to get back on their feet from the devastating effects of the war. Our neighbours were city office workers,

London, 1920

bank clerks, teachers with an occasional "lower middle class" such as policemen or railway workers.

"Class" was something that was taken for granted and people were carefully put in categories by their associates. My family would have been termed "middle class" verging up into "upper middle class" as Dad's job improved. We were very much aware of our family background. Dad's mother came from a farming background in Somerset and Dad had spent most of his childhood summers staying with cousins on their farm. His closest friend had been one of his cousins who had been killed in the war. Dad's father had been an orphan and was in the military and in his later years he became an alcoholic. Of course that word was never used but in my teens I heard mention of "Granddad's little drinking problem". To us, as children, his good points were always stressed, the fact that he was an excellent musician and played in the band of His Majesty's Coldstream Guards being pointed out to us.

Mum's family was very different. Her father was a solicitor and her forebears had been prominent in commerce and the navy. One ancestor had been an aide de camp to Queen Victoria and two admirals had played their part in British history, Admiral Drew and Admiral D'Horsey. There had been generations of wealth and position that had been lost when two brothers feuded over the business and in the process lost both the business and the money. Mum's father was also an accomplished musician having studied at the Conservatoire of Music in Antwerp where some of the family's remote connections had business. Granddad's full name was George William Schroder Bonner so I imagine the "Schroder" came from Antwerp somewhere along the line.

So we moved into our new house, our first house with electric lights as our former homes had always had gas lighting. A step up in the social scale, a fact that I did not hesitate to rub in when I visited my cousins who - poor things, I thought - still had the old fashioned gas lights. The house was of a more or less standard suburban design. This particular house was attached to others on either side but later homes, those that we owned were semi-detached, that is they were joined to another house on one side but not on the other. The houses were always built of brick with a slate roof. The plans were similar, a good sized entry hall with stairs leading to the second floor where there were three bedrooms, a bathroom, and a separate lavatory. Downstairs leading off the hall would be the kitchen, living room (sometimes called a lounge), and a dining room. The latter two rooms would both have coal burning fireplaces and the kitchen had a coke burning boiler that was never allowed to go out as in addition to providing heat in the kitchen it also heated our water supply for the kitchen and bathroom. Later houses we had, had electrically heated water tanks but still had the boiler for warmth in the kitchen. In the two larger bedrooms there would be sometimes a coal fire but more likely in the newer homes there would be an electric or gas wall heater. The third and smallest bedroom, always mine until Doug went to college, had no fireplace.

We had no major appliances that are standard today. Refrigeration was unheard of, not required by the climate and therefore sheer luxury. We had a pantry in the kitchen, a cupboard with a section of the outside wall open to the air, just covered with wire mesh and this allowed fresh air in to help preserve meats that were stored overnight. Shopping was

London, 1920

done every day except Sunday, my mother walking a mile or so to the nearest shop or bus route every day of her life and carrying home all the groceries.

Clothes were washed in a small "boiler", a sort of washtub heated either by coal or gas and ironing was done first by irons heated on the gas ring of the cooker and later by gas fired irons. My father and brother had to have a clean white shirt every day and after I left elementary school I had to have a white blouse every day so Mum was kept busy washing and ironing, no such thing as wash and wear. Lots of darning to do too, no nylon or polyester to last for ever, there were always piles of socks to be darned. All the white things were rinsed out in cold water with a "bluebag" in it. I still have no idea what the blue stuff was but it was a chunk of bright blue powdery stuff wrapped in a piece of muslin, turning the water bright blue and the clothes, apparently, white!

We had large gardens back and front that were always well kept up and presented a pleasant exterior appearance. Dad spent all of his spare time in the garden, he could grow anything and we always had lovely cut flowers in the house and home grown vegetables such as peas, beans, carrots, lettuce etc. I remember particularly his glorious sweet peas and pansies and the roses that lasted so that it was not unusual to have a rose bud or two on the Christmas table. Mum did not can or bottle things but she did put down beans in salt so that we could have them well into the winter months.

Food in those days was "good healthy nourishing" food, no-one had ever thought of dieting and women expected to get "middle age spread" with no worry about it. Most people got adequate exercise from the amount of walking they did. We never had a car and money being scarce short trips were made by Shank's pony rather than by bus. Often if we were out shopping with Mum we would be given the option of riding home on the bus or having the penny bus fare to spend as we liked. Needless to say we usually opted for the penny though to-day I often wonder how Mum had the energy to walk home the mile or so at the end of a hard day.

Breakfast for Doug and I would be cereal, probably porridge in winter and in the summer months a dry cereal; the only one I can think of was Force, a sort of wheat flakes with the well remembered slogan of "Force is the power that raises you" and a picture of a man, known as Sunny Jim, leaping over a fence. Later on a few more varieties came on the market but that was much later. With the cereal we would have bread and butter and perhaps a soft boiled egg, no toast in the mornings as there was no fire that early in the morning and a fire was needed for toast. Dad would have a bigger breakfast, always two fried eggs, bacon and bread fried in the bacon fat. Sometimes we would also have some fried tomatoes and if I had fried bread anytime I liked to put just a dash of Bovril on it to give it flavour, Bovril being a beef concentrate for flavouring gravies etc. English bacon was unlike the bacon used in America, that kind of bacon we called "streaky" because it had so much fat in it and that was only bought for cooking with liver or rabbit when the fat was needed. Our bacon was more like smoked ham, or what is called Canadian bacon in the States.

When Doug and I were in elementary school we carne home for a midday dinner and then after school we would have tea with Mum, bread and butter and jam, perhaps a

London, 1920

scrambled egg or sardines on toast or a kipper and then some cake. Dad always had a full meal when he got home from work about 6.30. When we were in secondary school it was too far for us to come home for lunch. They did have cooked meals at school but we could not afford them so we took sandwiches and then had a cooked meal when we got home. We ate with Mum and earlier than Dad did, partially so that we could be finished and get started on our homework and partially so that Dad could eat his meal in peace. No doubt about it, Dads were kings in those days.

Our main meal was always meat and potatoes and a vegetable though once in a while Mum would bring in fish and chips and in the summer months we would have a salad with tinned salmon or cold meats. We could only afford a joint (roast) once a week and this was always the "Sunday joint", something to look forward to. Most days dessert was a milk pudding of some kind, tapioca (ugh!) or semolina and in the colder weather a boiled suet pudding or sponge pudding but on the weekends when the whole family ate together then Mum would make fruit pies and serve them with hot custard. I get hungry thinking about it. Dad had a favourite dessert, bread and butter pudding. This consisted of slices of bread and butter cooked in a custard with raisins. I hated it and went without dessert on those days. Mum was a marvellous cook and a great one for making a lot out of a little too.

We had plenty of apples available all the year around and in the summer we had a lot of fresh fruit, all kinds of plums, berries and cherries as they came into season. My favourite berries were loganberries and I also loved blackcurrants, something I have never found in the States; at least on the west coast. My favourite plum came in September and was a greengage; never see those here either. Citrus fruit, of course, all had to be imported. Oranges were on the expensive side and were considered a treat, lemons were bought in the summer if a cheap batch could be found and lemonade was made for our summer drink. Cheaper oranges and in greater quantities came on to the market a few years later, just in time to disappear completely for six years in the war! Such items as grapes and peaches were strictly luxury items as they were all hot house grown. They were usually purchased as gifts for hospital patients and then it would be just one peach, no more. Bananas were plentiful and not too expensive. We used to pass a banana storage place on our way to the shops and when I went shopping with Mum on a Saturday morning she would sometimes give me a couple of pennies and I would go in and ask one of the men unpacking the crates if I could buy a banana. There was usually a call up to his buddy, "Gimme a banana for the nipper, Bill" and I would be given the largest, fattest one there. They would not want to take the money but Mum always insisted that they do so.

A big treat in the summer was an ice cream cone, or frequently an ice water cone. This was part and parcel of the fun of the summer holidays and an ice cream man came around the streets on a cycle with a large bin attached for the frozen delights. Mostly it was sticks of brightly coloured and flavoured iced water, sometimes ice cream cones and very occasionally for a super treat we would have a chocolate covered ice cream bar.

As to sweets (candies) we got that at the local sweet shop. Here we could spend our penny or ha'penny on an item of our choice, ten minutes to decide what we wanted and another minute watching the treat being weighed up and put

London, 1920

into a paper bag. There was a great selection, all kinds of toffees, hard boiled sweets and liquorice including a liquorice stick stuck in a small packet of sherbet, a pastel coloured, flavoured, slightly fizzy powder, fizzy that is when you ate it. There were humbugs and bulls eyes and jelly joojoobs, not to mention gob stoppers, so named because the ball of candy was so big that when you put it in your mouth - slang "gob" - it filled it up completely until a certain amount had been licked away.

There was much open country around us and a wooded area known as the Chislehurst Woods was not far off. We spent a lot of our free time rambling through the woods and playing games of our own devising. I would play with friends in their gardens or have them over to play in mine but Doug, being much older, would go off to the fields and play with his friends there, cricket or football depending on the season.

My brother was very good about playing with me, no doubt a little pressure was applied by my parents also, but until he was in his teens he shared games with me and abetted me in things I wanted to do. I remember one time when taking me along proved rather disastrous. He was going off to play a pick up game of football with some friends and Mum told him he had to take me with him. He was not too happy about the idea but told his friends he had to have his kid sister along and they could play while I had to stand on the sidelines, not get in the way and not be a nuisance. So I stood mutinously on the field wanting to get in the game and kick the ball too. The next thing I knew I was on the ground crying with a crowd of people around me. I had been hit in the head by a kicked football and knocked out for a moment. As soon as I came around a couple of adults who had been standing nearby told Doug to take me home right away and he did, grumbling at me all the way, mad that I had ruined his game and apprehensive as to the reaction of our mother. He used to get so mad at me at times but I cannot remember any real major fights. There probably were some but because he was five years older and a boy it was unthinkable that he should hit his little sister and I probably got away with murder more than once invoking my sex and frailty!

On rainy days, and there were lots of those, we played in doors. A favourite game at one time was "mountaineering". We would cover the stairs with cushions or pillows and using a walking stick of Dad's as an alpenstock would laboriously climb to the top with many a slip and tumble to the bottom of the stairs. Lots of imagination went into the game for somehow we never got to the top always being caught in an avalanche or a snowstorm with the peak just out of reach. One day instead of using the walking stick we usually played with Doug used another one and when Dad found out he was very angry and told us we were never to use that stick again. My brother knew why and, when my parents were not listening, told me the reason but I was a lot older before I was actually permitted to see that this stick was a sword stick. The handle unscrewed and there was a long deadly steel blade attached to the handle that slid into the hollow container. No wonder we were not allowed to touch it.

With my contemporaries I played the usual childhood games of make believe. I never liked dolls, had them from time to time but had no affection for them. Teddy bears were always a favourite toy and the Ted I had had since I was two was the love of my life. As a matter of fact I still have Ted, almost 76 years old now much the worse for wear and love

London, 1920

hugs. Mum replaced many a set of velvet paws and even added a velvet nose to keep in the stuffing! Years later when I left England Mum said that she kept the proverbial stiff upper lip losing her daughter - until she put Ted in the trunk. Then the tears came. But that is in the distant unimaginable future.

We had a dog, Bobby #3 I think, but no cat at this time. One thing we did have and in quantity were goldfish. The ragman used to wheel a barrow up the streets and cry out that he wanted old clothes. Mum would rustle up a couple of old shirts and in exchange the ragman would give us a goldfish – we supplied the jam jar. I presume if someone wanted money instead of a goldfish it could be negotiated but all I can remember is running out with the clothes and a jar and coming back bubbling with excitement clutching the jar now decorated by a goldfish. We transferred the new arrival to a fish bowl and sat back to admire him – or her. Of course they never lasted long, a week or so and we would find a body floating in the bowl, there would be a few tears and a ritual burial, usually in a cigarette box sometimes decorated with a purple cross and then the grave dug at one end of the garden. Before our tears were dry the ragman would be around again and the cycle started over.

In the evenings, after school work was done we relied on ourselves as a family group for fun and relaxation. During the long winter evenings we would play card games, listened to the gramophone and of course read for hours. I have vague memories of Dad bringing home our first wireless set. It was a large square wooden box and a big curving horn to go on top made of a brown sort of plastic. Of course the word plastic was not used, I think it was made of Bakelite. We children were warned on pain of the most dire consequences never to touch it. Dad did a lot of twiddling of the "cat's whiskers", something to do with it being a crystal set but to this day I am not sure exactly what he had to do to bring in the sounds of music and plays and news bulletins from London 2LO. Late afternoon was a special programme for children, "The Children's Hour". The people on this programme were known as Auntie This and Uncle That and they always used to finish the programme with an admonition to all the children listening and I have never forgotten it. "Now be good, not so good that everyone says, 'Now what is he up to' but just middling good". There was a children's club that you could join and I saved my pennies to join and got a badge - I still have it - that showed me to be a member of the B. B. C. Radio Circle, London branch.

Usually Mum would play cards with me while Dad read (lots of westerns!) and Doug did his homework, all gathered around the dining room table. We played games like "Snap" and "Beatcha neighbour outa doors", a rough translation of beating your neighbour so badly that he lost his home to you. Sometimes, especially on weekends, Friday and Saturday nights all four of us would play and then we might play pontoon or ving-et-un that Dad enjoyed. Mum used to tell us that during the war Dad had sent her home many packages of francs he had won playing cards but of course we never played for money, just counters. Doug and I played other games too. Snakes and ladders and draughts (checkers) and tiddley winks. I have no memory of this but I am told on one memorable occasion the remark was made at the end of the game that cheats never prosper. At this I piped up and said, "Yes they do because I'm prospering". This was when I was

London, 1920

barely old enough to know the meaning of the word "prosper" - so much for my early integrity!

My brother was now attending Eltham College, a secondary school to which he had obtained a scholarship. The school had originally been chartered as a school for the sons of missionaries and it still had quite a few boarders as well as the day students. It was a short bus ride away and Doug was very happy there. Incidentally the school battle cry at football matches etc. was "SSM! SSM!", short for "School for Sons of Missionaries".

My school was just a short walk away and there were many children in my age bracket living in the immediate neighbourhood. At one time there were three of us living in three adjoining houses with birthdays on three consecutive days, September 8th., 9th., and 10th., two of us the same age and one a year younger. Mum recalled one year when we each attended the other two birthday parties and on the fourth day all three of us were in bed with a bit of tummy trouble due to excitement and overeating.

I don't even remember the name of the girl who was the same age as myself but the one who was one year younger lived next door to me and I shall never forget her name, Marjorie Scott. Not that we were such good friends, in fact I began to dislike her immensely only because she was apparently a paragon of virtue. She was a tall thin redhead, her father an Irish policeman and her mother a Scot as was her maternal grandmother who lived with them. Marjorie, poor soul, had nothing to do with the feelings I had about her. I found her a bit insipid and very much in fear of her grandmother who ruled both Marjorie and her mother with an iron hand, but at home she was held up to me as a shining example. If I didn't practise my piano it would be, "I hear Marjorie playing every day". If I was very noisy and unladylike - a cardinal sin in those days - it was, "Marjorie does not act in that fashion" and if I did not get my homework done on time or did not get a good mark, "Marjorie really studies hard I am told". How I hated poor old Marjorie. I have not seen her or heard of her for over fifty years but I still shudder at the thought of her name!

We were all expected to behave well then, in fact we were trained to be "ladies and gentlemen". If I laughed too loudly I was reprimanded. I walked with no slouching and talked in a circumspect fashion but that does not mean that I was inhibited in having fun and I had as many loud chuckles as I wanted with Mum giggling along with me too. My brother was expected to take on the role of protector and helper if Dad was not there. When we were out walking he always took the outside, curbside, position if Dad was not with us, always raised his school cap if we passed a lady we knew. It was no hardship; just part of growing up and all our friends were similarly instructed. In many ways there was a lot to be said for it but, of course, much of it to-day is scorned by the women libbers as being demeaning. I beg to differ.

The small elementary school that I had been attending closed down and I had to go to a school about one and a half miles from home, taking the bus. A public bus, no school busses. I rather enjoyed it and did like the larger school; in summer I would sometimes save the bus fare and spend it on an ice cream cone and walk home with my friends. This, at one time, created some excitement for the family. Mum had gone shopping and as she had to change busses near the school she thought she would stop in there as it was time for

London, 1920

school to be let out, pick me up and then we could ride home together. She waited near the classroom and soon the doors opened and all the children came out - all but me. She then went in and asked the teacher about me and the poor woman could not remember me in the last session although she clearly remembered me in the session before that for that had been an exercise class in the school playground.

Instant panic, the headmaster was sent for, children were stopped and questioned, had anyone seen a strange man hanging around? Finally the police were sent for. Very shaken, Mum was put in the police car by a kindly Bobby who then drove her slowly along the bus route while they looked for me, checked the side streets and stopped and questioned older students.

I meanwhile was happily trotting along the last stretch of the walk home. I had completely forgotten the last session and seeing an open door out to the street at the end of the exercise class thought it would be a good joke to slip out that way instead of going into school and out the front door. This would give me a head start on my friends and I would surprise Mum by being home a bit early.

My memory fails me at this point, sufficient to say that I was in everyone's black books both at home and at school and I certainly got a lecture by the policeman pointing out what would happen to little girls who left school early. From early days we were taught to look on the police as friends. The policeman on the beat always said "Hello" as we passed him on the way to school and it was drilled into us that in any emergency we should go to the nearest policeman. When I was quite small I found a ring in the street walking home from kindergarten. I took it home and showed it to my mother who promptly put on her coat - and hat and gloves as always when leaving the house - and took me to the nearest police station. The find was duly logged in a big book by the policeman on duty, my name shown as the finder and I was told if the ring was not claimed by a certain length of time that I could claim it. The days passed so slowly I could hardly stand it but eventually the day arrived and I went back to the police station with Mum. The sergeant on duty checked the log and told us that the ring had not been claimed and it was mine. I had to write my name on a receipt and have it countersigned by Mum and went home with my ring in a rosy glow. Actually the ring was a rather cheap "mourning" ring and as Mum said "quite unsuitable for a child" so she gave me one of her own rings to wear "when I was older" and she kept the other ring although I never saw her wear it.

Years later I left a hockey stick in a phone booth near my school so the next day I went in to the police station to see if it had been handed in. It was there and I signed a receipt and was given the stick but not until after I was given a friendly talking to by the man on duty reminding me that I should take better care of the things my parents worked so hard to get for me. And he was so right about that, they could not afford a new hockey stick. Mum had had to run all over the place by bus and walk miles tracking down advertised second hand sticks until she found one for me that was in good shape and at a price she could afford. It would have indeed been a tragedy if I had lost it.

One of the drawbacks of living where we did was that we were a long way away from any good shopping centre. Having to shop every day this was not something to be taken lightly. There was a small group of shops with very limited

London, 1920

facilities a little over a mile away but it was an uphill walk on the way back when Mum would be carrying all the groceries and no easy bus service. To get to a better shopping centre it was a three mile or so bus ride and in addition to the time involved, the waiting around for busses in the inevitable rain there was also the cost of the bus fares to be considered. Dad had direct train service to the city from the station a mile away but it was a limited service.

We were also a long way from a chemist shop or a doctor although of course all doctors made house calls. Not that the doctor was very much of a consideration. You did not call on the doctor unless really needed, there were no such things as "checkups" and "shots". Dad was a great one for home remedies for preventative medicine. At regular intervals he would brew up a revolting tea made from senna pods and stand over us while we drank it, Doug stoically and quickly and me crying all the time and making the awful cupful last an hour. It was a laxative and supposed to "clean us out", well we never got sick so perhaps it worked. I shouldn't say never got sick as we did have the usual childhood things such as measles and mumps but we rarely got colds or flu. Of course a cold was not considered being sick, it was just a matter of taking another couple of handkerchiefs to school or work, you certainly did not skip either of these unless you were in the hospital and/or dying. One of Mum's cure-alls, considerably more gentle than the senna tea although I used to dislike it almost as much, was a bowl of bread and milk. It was exactly as the name implies, a bowl of warm sweetened milk with soggy pieces of bread swimming in it. Ugh!

Weighing the transportation problems and the fact that they were dissatisfied with the school I was attending my parents decided to try and move back near our former neighbourhood. A friend of Mum's owned some houses and one became available for rent so we moved into that. There was an elementary school about twenty minutes walk away for me and Doug was within easy reach of a bus to take him to Eltham College. There was some talk of him transferring to a closer school but he very much wanted to continue where he was so this was agreed to.

After the move we found that the house was not exactly as painted, in fact on closer inspection it left much to be desired. The previous tenants had left it very dirty and to accommodate the corner location of the house the living and dining rooms proved to be small and the whole house rather cramped. There was not much that could be done, rental homes were still scarce and so we were put on a waiting list for the next house that would become available and Mum set to, cleaned the house thoroughly and we learned to make do with the smaller rooms. There were three bedrooms but only one of them had a fireplace and two were extremely small.

The rather narrow staircase came down in the centre of the hall almost to the front door and I have a vivid recollection of coming downstairs one morning wearing a dressing gown and some woolly slippers that Mum had knitted for me. She was already at work with the carpet sweeper on the living room carpet. There was a bump in the corner of my slipper and all the way downstairs I was complaining about it, it was cramping my toes and was uncomfortable. Mum told me to sit down and eat my breakfast and stop grumbling, she had allowed me to sleep in on this Saturday as I had a bit of a cold and I suspect too so that she could get a head start on the housework in peace. I

London, 1920

ate, still grumbling, and then started to go upstairs to get dressed. Halfway up the stairs Mum could stand my fussing no longer, she sat me on the stairs and told me to give her the slipper so that she could see what was wrong. I did, and as I took the slipper off the lump came alive and a baby mouse who had settled in that nice warm place for a mouse snooze came tumbling out. Pandemonium! I screamed, Mum, startled, jumped back and fell over the carpet sweeper and the mouse took off to the farthest corner of the room. A lively chase ensued, Mum finally cornering the shivering little thing and pushing him into a paper bag to be released in the garden. To this day I can see myself and those pink woolly slippers.

Being so much closer to town and in an older suburb we did not have the open country around us as in our former house. We did have a large public park we called the "rec", short for recreation grounds. There was a river wandering through it and lots of grassy areas for impromptu games of cricket and soccer during the week and more formalised games for adults on Saturday afternoons. No playing on Sundays in those days.

So on the weekends or in the summer holidays all the neighbourhood children would go to the "rec" and play games of our own devising, no clubs or little league type of things in those days. The boys would make up games of football (soccer) or cricket depending on the season and the girls would usually get together and play rounders, not unlike baseball, or if they wee too young to enjoy that would play tag or just run around enjoying the freedom. The river was a great place to use our imaginations with all kinds of games. My brother and I would make paper planes, put a foreign stamp in as a pilot and then try and fly them down the small waterfalls inventing all kinds of catastrophes if the plane did not make it and fell in the water or, biggest excitement of all, was grabbed by a dog paddling in the river. The river itself was just a little creek, not deep enough for swimming and much too rough on the bottom for wading so in some areas, one in particular known as the "dog pond", dogs were allowed to frolic about.

On Saturdays some of the fathers would stroll down to watch a game or perhaps participate in it with their sons. Dad would love to lie on the grass watching while he would idly throw a ball for me to catch. It was quite a family affair although I don't know how much Doug really enjoyed, he never seemed as close to Dad as I was and for his part Dad never unbent very much with Doug, always the rather stern parent. Many years later when I was an adult I mentioned this to Mum and she said it had been very hard for both of them as Doug was almost five by the time Dad came back from the war and they had lost all those early years together that could never be recaptured. In fact she related a story that when Dad had reprimanded Doug over some small misdeed soon after Dad had come back into their lives Doug had gone running to Mum exclaiming that he didn't think they should keep Daddy as a pet as he really didn't like him much.

I remember one incident at the rec vividly. There had been a tree uprooted in a storm and it fell so that the upper branches lodged in the fork of another tree. I don't know how high it was; it was huge but I doubt now that I look back that the fork of the tree could have been much more than 15 feet off the ground. I was playing in the rec with Doug and some of his friends and my friends. I suppose I was about

London, 1920

nine or ten or so. All the boys began climbing the fallen tree by sitting astride the trunk and inching their way up to where it rested in the other tree. Soon I began bragging to my friends that I could do the same thing, no problem and then before I knew it there I was inching my way up and getting more scared every second. I made it up to the top and then panic set in and I was frozen there, unable to back down, unable to do anything but hang on and cry. Most of the kids faded away at this point, they were not going to be around when the inevitable adult would show up on the scene but of course Doug had to stay and he and his friends kept urging me to close my eyes and back down. Finally one of them had the bright idea to go up the tree and guide me down so he climbed up behind me and more or less dragged me backwards with both of us shaking all the way. Of course once I was on the ground I was all pride and boasting of my feat but I've never forgotten those terror stricken moments. I don't think my parents ever heard about that episode. Doug certainly would never tell them as he was supposed to be looking after his little sister and I wouldn't tell them because I knew I should never have climbed the tree.

The streets in the neighbourhood were lined with horse chestnut trees and in the summer the seed pods used to fall to the ground and the big polished chestnuts inside the pods littered the streets. They were not an edible chestnut and the children used to pick them up, drill a hole through them and put a piece of string through the hole, knotted at one end so that the string would not slip through. This was a "conker" and many challenges were made and taken up on the superiority of one's conker. They would be swung or flipped one against the other and a well aimed blow by your conker could split the opposing one wide open or chip it badly rendering it useless. With Doug teaching me some of the tricks of how to play conkers successfully I became quite a champion in my age group.

Another game we played - although our parents would have skinned us alive if they had known - was "knock down ginger". Best played on a winter day late in the afternoon when dusk came early. One of our group would ring someone's door bell and then we would run like the dickens and hide behind the hedge to see the unsuspecting householder come to the front door to answer the bell. I suppose that was the equivalent of today's kids calling on the telephone with wise remarks except that doing it in person presented a bit more of a hazard than the anonymity of the telephone. I mentioned hiding behind the hedge. Most older homes had fairly good sized gardens at the back of the house, a patch of lawn, some currant bushes and flower beds, but in the front of the house the gardens were smaller and almost always with a privet hedge across the front behind low iron railings, the hedge preserving the privacy of the front room windows that were fairly close to the street.

Life was not all play of course. The school day in elementary school was from nine in the morning until four or half past four in the afternoon and in high school the day was a little shorter although most of the days were extended to about the same time by the after school games programmes. Many high schools also required a half day attendance on Saturdays as did most business firms. After school there was homework every night; not just a nominal amount. By the age of eleven or so several hours were required.

London, 1920

There was never any question of any kind of entertainment except weekends or holidays, Monday through Fridays were school days and that was that. In the summer when the evenings were long we could play in the garden or in a friend's garden if close by but only after homework was done. Our summer holiday time was from the end of July to the end of August in elementary school and from the end of July to the middle of September in secondary school. At Easter we had two weeks holiday and the same amount of holiday at Christmas.

Our entertainments were simple. During school holidays Mum might take us to the pictures, the cinema, as movies were called then. We always got there early before the place opened so that we could get the cheap matinee price seats, often even cheaper for the first hour the cinema was opened. The programme always followed the same routine when I was small, first of all a newsreel then the main feature, a "lovey dovey" as we called it, usually pretty boring to me and then came some cartoons followed by a comedy or a cowboy epic.

By the time I was a teenager the lovey dovey and the cowboy had changed to two major features with the newsreel and cartoons in the middle; quite often with a stage show too. Stage shows could be anything from some dancers, magicians or jugglers to a full fledged mini ice show. We saw some people in these shows that went on to be famous in later years, one I particularly remember was the act of the Nicholas Brothers, not at the small local cinema but at a place closer to the centre of London, still a suburban theatre not in any way a major London show however.

Sometimes on Bank Holidays there would be special family all comedy shows. Normally on Bank Holidays we stayed home to avoid the crush but occasionally Dad would weaken and we all went to the pictures and laughed ourselves silly over Charlie Chaplin or Harold Lloyd. Sometimes to counteract the effect of three hours sitting we would go to a cinema some distance away and be prepared to either walk there or back to get some exercise. As Dad usually suggested a short cut and his shortcuts were notorious for getting us lost we were lucky if we got to the cinema on time or got home before dark. We usually did, though, because we always left ourselves with plenty of time, punctuality being a much praised virtue.

Another holiday treat was a visit to aunts and cousins. This was usually a whole days jaunt as Mum's sisters all lived in the other side of London. They all had several children both boys and girls close to my age so it was always fun to get together with them. It always had to be prearranged by letter as no one had phones back then so it was not unusual for it to be pouring with rain on the planned day but we took that in stride, grumbled of course but then we were used to wet summers.

I used to enjoy the journey, it was a long bus ride to town, about an hour, but much cheaper than train. Then we had to cross town, again usually by bus but sometimes on the underground. Then we would pick up another bus or train and so to my aunt's house. Quite often another aunt who lived nearby would come over too with her children so that the three sisters could get together at one time. I was fascinated by the streets of central London, there were still a lot of horse drawn vehicles around, delivery vans etc. and sometimes they would be drawn up to a horse trough for the horses to take a long drink. These large stone troughs were all

London, 1920

over London although they were no longer to be seen in the newer suburbs.

Sometimes we would take the bus through Blackwall tunnel to cross under the Thames. Its walls and ceiling were of shiny white brick and I always had the notion that there was just the thickness of one brick between us and the river so it was sort of a pleasurable but scary trip. Suppose that one brick fell out! One time, when I was a bit older and after much pleading with Mum we actually walked through the tunnel. The pavement was very narrow, we had to go in single file and the walls of the tunnel were curved up to the roof so when a double-decker bus went by you felt as if it was toppling over towards you. There were two or three gigantic fan areas and the machinery was very noisy. Add to this the noise of the traffic in the closed atmosphere and it did not exactly make for pleasant walking. Well anyway we did it - once was enough!

Dad was not a very gregarious sort of person so we did not have what today we would call "family" friends. Of course in those days everything was so much more formal, my parents calling their neighbours "Mr" and "Mrs" even after they had known them for years and there was no casual visiting back and forth as there is today. People were not unfriendly, many a friendly chat being held over the garden fence while the washing was being hung on the line or the fathers were working in the garden but there was a reserve and a keeping of each family to themselves, perhaps just a visit for a drink of good cheer at Christmas or some other special occasion.

Another thing we did, this more with Dad's side of the family as they lived nearer, was to have a musical evening together. Both of Dad's two sisters played the piano and Dad had a good bass singing voice. I can remember two songs from his repertoire, "The Lost Chord" and "The Deathless Army". As I grew older I used to wonder why we never heard some of the still popular wartime songs like "Pack up your Troubles" but Dad never sang those. He was not a very talkative person and I really doubt that he even talked to Mum much about it but I think he had some really terrible experiences in his years in the trenches and that he kept his thoughts about them firmly at bay. Many years later when he was an air raid warden in the second war I heard him joke and laugh about the "other war" with the men his own age and now his companions in the second world madness.

There would also be musical afternoons just for the four of us when Doug and I were expected to play the piano for Mum and Dad. Rather to my brother's amazement I decided to cash in on this. I would on occasion inform my parents that we had prepared a concert, or perhaps a play we had written, and I would make up a programme decorating it with cut outs from magazines etc. and then I would sell the programme to Mum and Dad at a penny each. They went along with the game, dutifully buying the programme and sitting through the entertainment.

As these entertainments were usually in the winter on a Sunday afternoon, if we were lucky we would end with the sound of the "muffin man" being heard and if we begged hard Mum would give us some money and we ran down the street after him, stop him and buy some crumpets for tea. He walked the streets on Sunday afternoons carrying a cloth covered tray on his head and ringing a bell while he cried "muffins, crumpets" as he went. Nothing in the world tasted

London, 1920

as good as those crumpets toasted on an open coal fire and dripping with butter. This was a special treat as there was little money to spare for things like this and the food budget had to go a long way and be spent mostly on necessities. Another big treat to us as kids were the hot cross buns on Good Friday. They were ordered in advance and were delivered hot from the bakery very early on Good Friday morning, left wrapped up on the doorstep before most people were even up. Good Friday was a bank holiday so everyone was home and no shops were open.

Of course most Sundays we were not having family entertainment as we were packed off to Sunday school at the nearest Church of England church. I had a sneaking hunch even back then that this was more to give Mum and Dad a peaceful Sunday afternoon than to give us any religious instruction!

I don't think Dad's family had any particular religious affiliation, nominally I suppose they were Church of England. My mother's family had been high church and there is even a family crypt in the churchyard of a London church where one family member a generation ago had been vicar but Granddad had turned Catholic in his youth and had of course required his wife to change also and to bring the children up in the Catholic faith. My mother had left the church as soon as she became an adult but one of her sisters was a nun and Mum and Dad had followed their civil marriage by a church wedding at a later date to keep peace in the family. I attended many Catholic services too when I was older and stayed overnight with my cousins but I never felt drawn to the ritual although I was never told anything adverse by Mum; just that I should go to each church and make up my own mind.

Mum's parents lived "at the seaside", at Brighton on the south coast and usually in the summer months we would go and visit them for a day. Most often we went on a Sunday as that was the day that the railways put on cheap excursion fares and as almost everyone worked a half day on Saturday the big relaxation day was Sunday.

It was quite an event, first of all up extra early and the walk, a mile or so depending on where we lived at the time, to the railway station where we would catch the suburban train to central London. From there we would walk or possibly take a bus to the main railway terminal that served Brighton, usually Victoria Station. Electric service back then was only for short local travel so the trains to the coast were still steam trains and I can remember the exciting smell in the railway station, trains pulling out bellowing black smoke and others sitting waiting for passengers but still emitting wispy trails of smoke from time to time. There were crowds of people all cheerfully heading for a day at the beach or, if they were lucky, starting off a week's holiday, small children carrying their toy shovels and pails to use to dig on the beach and harassed parents trying to keep an eye on their families. Truth to tell the beach at Brighton was all pebbles, very little sand, but hope sprang eternal in the young breasts.

Dad would plunge ahead of us and find room in a carriage and we would bustle in hopefully getting at least one seat with the back to the engine so that Mum could sit without getting soot in her eyes when the window was open - and the window was always open, devils for fresh air, the

London, 1920

English. When we went through a tunnel Dad would spring up and close the windows but otherwise they stayed open.

Of course we never realised, what child did, how hard Mum had worked the day before getting everything ready. We took lunches with us and not just sandwiches but home made meat pies, home made cake and usually some lemonade to wash it down. Clean, neat clothes, it was not the thing to wear "grubbies" even if you went to the beach. Dad had a clean shirt and tie, probably a lightly striped or figured shirt to show that this was a casual day, and of course he would have the inevitable jacket. My brother would be in shorts, also with shirt and tie and high socks and I would be wearing a neat dress as would Mum. White socks for me and hat and gloves for Mum.

We always felt slightly superior to the "day trippers" - were we not going to visit relatives, not just to sit on the beach? My grandparents were in their sixties but to me they seemed very old. Granny always wore very long dresses, she was a true lady in every meaning of the word and had never worked outside her home. She spoke very quietly and around her we children were always on our very best behaviour. One of my aunts, widowed in the war, lived with her parents and always after the big high tea when we were thinking about catching the train back to London she would disappear and return with a stick of Brighton rock for us. This was edible rock, a candy bar of hard candy with the name of the town "Brighton" right through it so that even when we licked off the very last piece the name still showed, red on the white candy. These sticks came in different flavours and different sizes but we usually had one in peppermint and about eight inches long.

So back home, the last leg of the journey done in darkness and after the walk from the station the house always seemed so very welcoming. Before we had left that morning everything, books, pencils, homework etc. that would be required for school on Monday morning had been laid out in readiness - a habit that persists to this day. Even now if I know I am going to be late home on Sunday I get organised for Monday morning work. My mother would be proud of me!

Shops stayed open every night until seven or eight and usually later on Saturdays but nothing was open on Sunday. One day during the week they closed at 1:00 p.m., on Saturdays in the heart of London and on either Wednesday or Thursday in suburban areas. The boundaries for each day were clearly set, all the shops in a particular area closing on the same day. I remember at one time one of the selling points of our house was that we lived on the dividing line of Wednesday and Thursday closing so in effect we could have shops open all week.

Among the main streets of shops in most of the older communities were street hawkers who parked their barrows in the streets and sold fruits, vegetables etc. at competitive prices. Quite often there would also be a small open air market area where all these street vendors could set up their stalls on a temporary basis. Sometimes the stalls would be there permanently but empty of goods except on certain days, this being part of the tradition of the open air markets still found today in country towns where goods are brought in for sale from surrounding farms and where the markets then even include livestock.

London, 1920

It was always a treat to go shopping with Mum on a Saturday evening. On a cold winter night the market was lit with gas flares that cast a glow over everything and made the shadowy forms of both sellers and shoppers seem exciting and mysterious. And there was often a "hot chestnut man" who had a small brazier with red hot coals on one side of his barrow and he would roast chestnuts and sell them by the bagful. The glow and heat from the brazier were part of the enchantment of the winter scene too, from my point of view as a child. I doubt my mother thought of shopping for the family in a very romantic light.

Not only were the stalls and open markets fascinating. I used to like the atmosphere of the ordinary shops too. Suburban shops with several departments but very modest by today's department store standards, were always quiet and rather dignified, the assistants courteous and helpful always addressing Mum as "madam". And there was always a black suited gentleman, the floor walker, in the background to give help if needed. One of the things I most wanted to be when I grew up was a cashier in a large shop. The cashier sat in a little box above the floor of the shop, usually in a central location, and she made change for all the shop assistants all over the various departments. Every assistant when she took the money from a customer wrote up a sales slip and put it with the money into a little round container that would then be screwed into a socket above her head. With a tug of her hand this container would zing across the floor on wires right into the cashier waiting in her little box. The cashier would make change, receipt the customer's sales slip and return the whole thing to the waiting assistant. What power, I thought, to sit there in charge of all the money and send little boxes winging across the floor in all directions. That was the job for me.

Talking of shops I remember that on Christmas Eve all the shops used to stay open until eleven at night and it was part of the Christmas excitement to go out late in the evening to buy some last minute gift with Dad. When I talk about late in the evening I mean about nine o'clock or so so that we could be back and safely tucked into bed before too late.

I remember one year when I was about six or seven my brother had gone out early in the day by himself and bought a present that was to be our joint gift to Mum. It was a "crystal" bowl bought at Woolworths and after showing it to me in the secrecy of his bedroom he put it in a paper bag and tossed the bag over to crimp the corners as he had seen shopkeepers do with bags of sweets. Calamity! The bag dropped and the bowl was smashed. My parents of course heard the crash and knowing full well what was going on my Dad came in pretending Mum did not know anything was amiss. He asked how much the bowl cost and said if we were quiet and kept the secret he would go out now and buy a replacement bowl, it was about eight o'clock in the evening then. I piped up that it had cost us sixpence as I had contributed threepence but Doug said it actually cost a little more as he had put in a few extra pennies without asking me to increase my share - that was a big brother for you. So Dad left his nice warm hearth and book and went out in the freezing cold to make the purchase. I never did wonder why Mum would not have an inkling as to what was going on. The replacement bowl - definitely not bought at Woolworth's - was in use fifty years later.

London, 1920

Christmas was a very special time. Until we were in our teens no decorating was done until after we children were in bed on Christmas Eve so we went to bed full of anticipation but the house quite bare of decoration except perhaps a few paper chains we might have made at school. Dad would hang paper decorations in the living and dining rooms, the same ones year after year, very familiar and the essence of Christmas to us. Our stockings of course were hung on Christmas Eve.

On Christmas morning, we awoke early of course and Mum and Dad would call us into their bedroom. Dad would set about making a cup of tea for Mum and we would snuggle into bed with her. Then Dad would bring out the gifts one by one and we would open them on the bed with much excitement. Then downstairs to exclaim over the look of the rooms and find out that goodies had been left in our stockings. There were usually nuts and sweets and often the whole thing topped with a tangerine. Tangerines were only available at the Christmas season and were a real treat.

In the morning while Mum fixed the Christmas dinner Dad usually took Doug and I out for a long walk. I am sure at times it must have been pouring with rain and we did not go but I seem to remember most Christmas days as very cold but sunny good days for walking. Then back to a festive dinner, usually a roast of pork, very occasionally a turkey if we could afford one, or sometimes a goose. Of course we always finished up with Christmas pudding with hot custard sauce and hopefully we found a thr'penny bit in the pudding. Amazing how often both of us ended up with one even if Mum and Dad found one in their pieces less often!

After dinner we would play with our toys while Mum and Dad had a rest then Dad would pitch in with help from us when we were older and we would get the dinner things all cleared away. While we were doing this Mum would get the tea table laid, an especially lovely cloth and the best china. We rarely had a large tree, they were too expensive as they had to be imported from Scandinavia or Germany in most cases, but we had a miniature artificial tree and this was the centrepiece of the tea table with little gifts on it. And at each place would be a "bonbon" or "cracker", the pull apart paper rolls that had a tiny fire cracker in them so that when they were pulled apart there was a flash and a bang. They had paper hats and little toys inside them so our Christmas tea was always a lot of fun. Nothing especial to eat, our usual tea fare of bread and butter and jam but we did finish up with a lovely Christmas cake, a rich fruit cake topped with a thick layer of marzipan and then decorated with icing and a Father Christmas or perhaps a snowman. I was never very fond of the fruit cake but I adored the marzipan so I would gobble the cake down quickly and then linger over every lovely mouthful of the almond richness.

The day after Christmas was also a bank holiday, the day being know as Boxing Day, the traditional day for the giving of Christmas "boxes" to those who served you throughout the year. For us, as kids, it was always the day when we sat down right after breakfast and wrote all our "thank you" letters to aunts and cousins for the gifts we had received. If you had five handkerchiefs, one each from five aunts, you had to write a thank you letter to each one expressing the thought that without their handkerchief your life would have been incomplete. Only after all the gifts had been acknowledged

London, 1920

could you relax and enjoy the rest of the day playing with the things you had received and looking forward to the rest of your holiday from school.

Mary Datchelor Girls' School, 1931

Soon after the second Christmas in this house I realised that the critical scholarship phase of my school life was just around the corner. The big event in an English schoolchild's life was the examination that had to be taken between the ages of ten and eleven. The results of this exam had a big effect on your life. If you passed this exam you were awarded a place in a secondary school with the advantages of a better and lengthier education. If you failed you continued at the elementary school for two more years when you had one more chance at the exam. If you failed again then you stayed at the same school and your formal education was over at age fourteen or fifteen and you had to find a job with the limited education you had. The secondary school leaving age was sixteen or seventeen and then you would be equipped to get a good job or continue to university if you wanted to enter one of the professions. The secondary school education was as good as most of the college courses are today and only the major professions such as medicine required further education. Such fields as banking, librarianship etc. were learned on the job obtained by the matriculation certificate from the secondary school. Teaching required a two year additional course unless you wished to teach on university level.

So with the scholarship on my horizon there was a lot of extra studying every evening. Mum and Dad coached me in

Mary Datchelor Girls' School, 1931

their spare time, listening to the things I had to learn by heart and making sure that I understood everything that I read. These examinations at a fairly early age have had their critics on the grounds that it required too much strain on the part of young children but it was an effort shared in most cases by the entire family and the sense of accomplishment was great. I think the young thrive on pressure rather than the general indifference that they feel today knowing that they will automatically go from one grade to another whether they work hard or not and that they will graduate from high school regardless of their knowledge.

In my case with a lot of hard work and a lot of family support plus the usual little bit of luck that goes with all things I did pass the exam. I can remember the day that I heard that I had passed and been awarded a scholarship. There were eight of us who had passed out of a class of about twenty five and the lucky ones were allowed to leave class early so that we could hurry home and tell our parents. One of my friends was ill and as she had passed also I detoured on my way home to tell her mother. She was so thrilled she gave me a piece of cake and a penny and a big hug then I ran, and I mean ran, home to tell Mum. What a day that was. Mum was so happy and Dad and my brother were equally excited.

Next we had to decide at which school I might take up the scholarship. There were government run schools who were obligated to take any scholarship student and then there were privately endowed schools who took mostly fee paying students but accepted a certain number of scholarship pupils. These schools had stiff entrance examinations to determine which of the scholarship applicants they wanted to accept but on the whole they gave slightly better education than the state schools.

Mum and Dad decided that I should try for one of the private schools and we applied for admittance to the entrance exam. More swotting (working hard at studies), more pushing, but I did get through and so I could look forward to starting at the Mary Datchelor Girls' School & Training College in September 1931, a few days after my eleventh birthday.

That summer was a happy one for me, a feeling of success and approval by my parents and happy anticipation of a whole new life opening up. Mum organised the usual summer holiday treats and one day stands out in my mind, not because it was really so special but it typifies the sort of carefree and happy days we had that summer. Doug had long wanted some billiard cues as he had learned to play billiards at a friend's house. We had pockets that screwed on to the table and webbing that stretched from one pocket to another to act as the cushion but no cues. Mum told us one morning that she thought it was just possible that we could find some cues at a second-hand shop and she also thought the budget would stretch to them so we set out by bus for a neighbourhood not too far away but one that had several second-hand shops and street stalls. Near the street market we did find many shops and had a great time going in and out and checking for what we wanted. It took a while and we looked at many shops but finally we found just what we wanted, not only two cues but a professional looking score board with pegs that slid along to keep score. Mum decided that the price was satisfactory so we bought them and set off back to the bus stop. Doug and I each carried one cue and at each street lamp we would

Mary Datchelor Girls' School, 1931

pretend that we were lamp lighters until Doug got a bit carried away in his excitement and jumped up on the base of a lamp in his role of lamplighter. That was enough, said Mum and from then on we walked more circumspectly. I should explain that at this time all the street lights were gas lit and each day at dusk a man walked along the street with a long pole to switch on each lap, one at a time. Hence our game with the billiard cues.

Soon after this we moved again to another house, just about a mile away, a house similar to the one we had just left but larger and more pleasantly situated. It was still a rental but Mum and Dad were both striving towards the day when we could own our own home and sometimes on a Saturday we would take a bus ride into the country and have a little walk when we got there - there were always pleasant lanes and woodland paths to wander through - but I realise now that they were spying out the land and looking for areas that would be close enough to town for Dad and our schools but far enough out of town to have houses with prices within our reach. Of course in those days such moves were never discussed with "the children" we were simply presented with the fait accompli and we had no idea what prompted the move, whether it was economic (better or worse!), transportation problems or other reasons.

This year turned out to be a bad one for Doug. He had been helping Dad in the garden of the house we had just moved into and following a stench in one corner of the garden they found the decomposed body of a cat not far from the surface of the garden. They dug it up and Dad disposed of it but some of Doug's friends came by and he went off to play with them without thinking to go in the house and wash his hands before he left. A few days later he became ill and the dread - before penicillin - word "septicaemia" was heard. In all probability Doug had had a small open cut on his hand and had got some of the decomposed cat or dirt in the wound and it had then turned septic. In those days this was nearly always fatal and it was a very worried household for several days until he turned the corner. We did not go to hospital but the doctor came every day and tried various remedies. Whether from those or Mum's common sense handling he did recover but he was out of school for several weeks and remained rather tired and run down.

Not long after this, undoubtedly due to his weakened condition Doug caught diphtheria, again at that time a dreaded disease. This time he had to go to the hospital and the local health authorities came to the house and took away his bedding to be sterilised. I remember Mum almost crying over the state of the mattress when it was returned. Doug himself recovered very quickly but his throat cultures continued to show positive and they would not let him out on the unsuspecting public as he was still a carrier of the disease. Eventually he was transferred to a convalescent home and he rather enjoyed it as he felt fine and had the run of the place becoming quite a pet of the nurses.

Mum of course did not feel so fine about it, he was still missing school and no one could give her any idea as to how long he would be in quarantine. The convalescent home was a long way from our home but one day Mum decided that she wanted to see where it was. She made some cakes etc. to take to Doug and she and I set out. It was a long bus ride and after we left the bus it was a long walk to the gates of the

Mary Datchelor Girls' School, 1931

home. At the gate we were met by a guard who phoned in to check the situation. "Sorry, no visitors". Poor Mum, we left the box of goodies and turned around for the walk back to the bus and then home. In retrospect one wonders why a phone call was not made before leaving home to check on the possibility of visiting but the average person just did not use the phone as it is used today, it was meant for emergencies only and in any case one did not want to bother the poor nurses unnecessarily.

When Doug finally got home it was decided that he should transfer to a school nearer home. He was very unhappy about it and never felt part of that school as he did at Eltham College but I suppose the decision was made for two reasons. He had lost half a year of school now and would have a hard time catching up but the nearer school had slightly lower academic standards so catching up would be easier. Also after bouts of illness so close to each other it was felt that he should not have to tackle such a long journey to school each day.

Meanwhile I was settling in at Datchelors. The journey to school was by bus, half a mile walk to the bus stop and then about a half hour ride. As we got closer to the school more and more students got on the bus. All schools had distinctive school uniforms so we were easy to spot. The standard uniform was a drill slip, a loose tunic hanging in pleats from a low square yoke. Underneath this was a long sleeved white blouse with the school tie. Our drill slips were navy as most schools were and our school colours being gold and blue the tie was striped in those colours. We wore black stockings and black oxfords. When we reached the exalted Upper Fifth class, age 15 - 16, then we could dispense with the drill slip if we wished to and wear a navy blue skirt with the regulation blouse and tie. The black stockings were still required of course. Travelling to school we wore navy coats and a navy blue felt hat with the gold and blue band on it and a school badge in the front.

In the summer term Datchelors had an unusual policy for girls schools at that time. We could wear cotton dresses, uniform of course, but in a choice of six pastel colours. They all had white collars and cuffs on the short sleeves and at the neck a short black bow. A department store near the school stocked all the uniforms for many schools and also had material available if we wished to have the summer dresses made at home. In the summer we wore navy blazers with the school crest on the pocket and a panama hat with the school band and badge. As the school was governed by the ancient guild the Worshipful Company of Clothworkers the school badge was the crest of the Company and our motto their motto "Amor vincit omnia", love conquers all – a great motto for a girl's school.

Actually the school had not started as a girls school at all. Mary Datchelor and her husband lived in London and in 1699 when she died she left three unmarried daughters, one of whom was also called Mary. This daughter died in 1726 and among her many bequests made provisions for apprenticing yearly two poor children from the income of the houses she owned at her death. A hundred years later the trustees finally sold the property and invested the proceeds in annuities at the then amazing rate of 3%. There were at that time, about 1870, no schools providing advanced education for girls and the trustees decided to use the funds for that purpose and they established the school. One other girls

Mary Datchelor Girls' School, 1931

school was opened shortly before Datchelors but when it opened in 1877 it became the second oldest girls high school in the country. The Clothworkers Guild became trustees of the endowment and governors of the school in 1894 and a few years after that the curriculum was extended so that the school also became a training college for teachers. The school was to last about a hundred years after that until preferring "death to dishonour" they gave up their identity and merged with another endowed school rather than lower their educational standards to comply with the London County Council's requirements for funding. The L.C.C. at that time, in common with their U.S. counterparts having decided that equal education for everyone meant bringing everyone down to a certain level rather than raising everyone's sights.

As I mentioned the journey to school at that time was always by bus. The busses were double-deckers and as enclosed upper decks were just beginning to be used most of the busses had open upper decks. In view of the wet climate there were tarpaulin covers for the seats and it was a great game for us to run up the stairs and hide under the cover hoping to get away with not paying the fare. As the bus conductor obviously saw us board and go upstairs and as we could not vanish into thin air from the top of the bus it was rather a wasted effort but we kept trying and were always surprised when the conductor - surprisingly patient most of the time - caught us in our attempt to cheat.

The first year at Datchelors the curriculum consisted of the basics of English, arithmetic, history and geography. On the lighter side were music appreciation, art, needlework, gymnastics and domestic science.

I had no trouble with the more important subjects although it was a new experience for me to be so strictly graded. My English teacher, Miss Gaster, would deduct marks if I failed to put a full stop after my name at the top of my paper or if I forgot to put in a comma when dating anything but after a few weeks of this I never forgot again. I was also fairly good in arithmetic and history and geography presented no particular problems at this stage of the game. My art teacher quickly realised she had no Rembrandt on her hands but I got by and thanks to my guardian angel my sewing teacher, Miss Rivers, was a dear lackadaisical soul who just cried quietly to herself when she looked at my appalling efforts.

Domestic science, the forerunner of home economics, was fun. We had to wear white overalls and we made lots of little useless cakes and listened to lectures on how to run a house based on the assumption that we would all eventually own a home equipped with all the necessary servants and therefore needed to know how to handle a domestic staff. Of course at that time that was not too far fetched, many of the girls did have servants in their homes and the eventual goal for all women was a home and family. Our Headmistress had a doctor of literature degree from Cambridge and her main aim was to turn out women capable of thinking for themselves and entering a profession but one who would also be able to run a home should she decide on marriage instead of a career. It was most unlikely that a woman should have both a home and a career, I cannot remember any of our teachers being married.

I enjoyed gym too although I was not exactly an athletic star. The general term of "gym" encompassed both the

Mary Datchelor Girls' School, 1931

regular classes in gymnastics and the voluntary - more or less - games participation. Gymnastics in the first year were mostly exercises known as "physical jerks". For some reason after the American invasion ten years later this term disappeared! Then after the basics we progressed to rope climbing and the balance beams and vaulting horse. As for games as we were a city school our playing fields were a long way away and so we went after the regular school hours once or twice a week taking a bus or walking the couple of miles. In winter we played hockey and lacrosse and in summer tennis and cricket and rounders.

In the second year our studies were extended to include French and Latin, physics and botany. Arithmetic took a back seat while we began algebra and later geometry. These subjects continued with only minor changes, such as chemistry replacing physics, for the next five years.

I remember one offshoot of our first French lessons. At lunch time the youngest ones of us in school used to play a wild game called "Help". I don't remember the details of the game but it did involve tearing up and down stairs and yelling and more often than not bumping into older students or staff members who were trying to go about their own business. After a few days of this D. B. (short for Dr. Dorothy Brock, the Headmistress) banned the game of "Help" so with what we thought was great ingenuity we came up with the French "Au Secours" and went on with the game. After morning assembly and prayers the next day, always a time for important announcements that affected the whole school, we were told in no uncertain terms that the game whether known by the word for help in French, German, Spanish, Italian, Latin or Greek was forbidden. A few brave spirits did think of "Aid" but most of us got the point and the game was dead.

So the days went by in a normal routine marked by holidays and other special days throughout the year. In the spring there was a lot of excitement on Boat Race Day. This was the day that the universities of Oxford and Cambridge raced each other on the Thames in the culmination of a week of rowing events. The whole nation took sides and for weeks before everyone would be buying favours to wear or wearing bows of ribbon, pale blue for Cambridge and royal blue for Oxford. Mum and Dad and Doug were all for Oxford so probably out of cussedness, or maybe just because I liked the pale blue colour I was a Cambridge backer. Cambridge never seemed to win so I was always the underdog and gloomy for days afterwards but once every few years Cambridge would win and then I was so proud you would think I had done the rowing instead of just listening to the event on the radio.

Easter holiday was a happy time. Good Friday and Easter Monday were public holidays so that it was a long weekend for Dad as well as a week off school for Doug and I. The weekend started with the delivery of Hot Cross Buns to our house early in the morning by the baker. They were really hot, just out of the oven and we would have them for breakfast, sometimes as a treat having breakfast in bed when Dad brought Mum up her early morning cup of tea. We did not attend any kind of religious services but Mum felt that Good Friday should be a rather quiet day. Years later I made a date with a girl friend to go to the cinema on Good Friday and Mum remonstrated with me, saying that she thought that was one day when we should not be going out for that kind of entertainment. I pointed out that she did not object to my

Mary Datchelor Girls' School, 1931

brother going off to play in a rugby match on that day so why couldn't I go to the cinema? After a bit of thought she acknowledged that I had a point and I went off with my friend but Mum was still a bit unhappy about it. Easter Sunday was the day for chocolate eggs and bunnies and when we were older we used to give Mum and Dad some sort of chocolate gifts too.

In the autumn the big day was November 5th., Guy Fawkes day. No school holiday or bank holiday but a big evening. For days ahead there would be children standing on street corners (needless to say we were never allowed to do this) with a home made effigy and a box in front with a slot and a sign saying "Spare a penny for the guy". People would drop in a few pence for the purchase of fireworks for the big day. And everywhere we went we heard the chant:

"Remember, remember the fifth of November
Gunpowder, treason and plot
I see no reason, why gunpowder and treason
Should ever be forgot"

For the uninitiated I should point out that Guy Fawkes was a man who tried to blow up the Houses of Parliament in 1605, the explosion set to go off on November 5th. He spent the year before tunnelling under the House of Lords and storing gunpowder there ready for the big day but the day before he was to put the plan in action the plot was discovered. He was caught and executed but the day of the plot is celebrated with firework displays and in every back garden Dads all over the country tried to set off Catherine wheels and rockets. I say "tried" because November 5th. was invariably soggy and damp or pouring with rain. If all the fireworks sputtered out in the rain we would go inside and light up some sparklers to try and offset the disappointment.

Fog was with us a lot in November. Today it would be called smog, it was a mingling of the November heavy mists and the smoke from thousands of coal burning fireplaces. I have been in a bus when the conductor had to get out and guide the driver along at a snail's pace with a flashlight and one time the fog seeped into the cinema so thickly that we could not see the screen and we had to call off the show and get our money back. I always found fog rather exciting, after all I did not have to drive in it and it was rather spooky and Sherlock Holmesy. When I began to travel to school on the train I found it was not such fun, the trains would crawl along, setting off the fog warnings placed on the rails and suddenly a train would pass us on an adjoining line, no sound, no warning, suddenly it was there and gone. Quite scary and it meant I would be late home with the walk from the station rather scary too.

Just before my third year in Datchelors we moved again, out of London to the small town of Beckenham in the county of Kent. I came to love this house dearly and was very happy there although it did have drawbacks in being a long way from the rest of my friends. This was the first house that we had owned and it was a definite step up in the social scale, a much nicer neighbourhood. The biggest snag was that it was a long way from the nearest railway station, the busses and shops. As I was at school on a scholarship before the move was finalised Mum had to talk to the London County Council Board of Education. So she took the bus and went up to County Hall and spent most of the day being shunted from one department to another. The upshot of the various

Mary Datchelor Girls' School, 1931

discussions was that although I was moving out of their jurisdiction my scholarship to the school in London would still be valid.

I think we all enjoyed the new house. The street was a cul de sac and our house was on the end of the road so that we were adjacent to the playing fields that belonged to one of the big five banks. On Saturdays I used to like to stand and look out of the window on the landing on the stairs and watch cricket matches or football matches depending on the season.

At this time we had a dog, Bobby. As I look back we seem to have had several "Bobbys" although what actually happened was that we lost two puppies in rather quick succession, victims of distemper, medical science for animals being no better in those days than it was for humans. Then we had a black and white fox terrier, the dog we had in the house in Beckenham. After his death we had a black and tan terrier who was with us until the start of the war in 1939. But I'm getting at ahead of myself, nothing was farther from my thoughts in my early teens than a world war. We had grown up hearing our parents talk about THE WAR but that was for our parents to talk about not for us to experience.

Bob used to sit in our garden and listen with cocked head to the shouts and laughter coming from the other side of the fence. He expressed his disapproval in no uncertain terms when a cricketer climbed over our fence one day to retrieve a ball. Dad had to rescue the man from Bob standing stiff legged and snarling but not before Dad had given the man a lecture about trespassing whether to collect a ball or not. After that the players were a little more pleasant if they needed help and one summer they even asked Mum and I to attend their summer fete day in exchange for us allowing them to run their radio off our electricity for a couple of hours.

This was the first time that Dad had been able to start his garden from scratch and he loved that place, the flower beds, the fruit bushes and vegetable beds at the end of the garden away from the house and of course his pride and joy, his lawn.

Talking of lawns that reminds me. One time when Mum and Dad were out Doug and some of his friends had the bright idea of moving our large antique oak dining room table out on to the lawn to give lots of elbow room for a game of billiards or ping pong. At the end of the day it was taken back in the house and everything tidied up. Dad came home and raised Cain asking who had moved the table outside. We could not understand how Dad got to be so clairvoyant until he pointed to the lawn and there on his pet lawn was a large circular track worn almost down to mud with so many feet walking around the table all day. Parents are so omnipotent!

Mum also enjoyed having her own house and not being under the thumb of a landlord. One of the things she wanted to do was to enclose the front porch on one side, partly for the look of the thing and partly to prevent the rain blowing in on the front door step. She thought a window in there, preferably not clear glass, would do the trick so she kept looking and had the measurements in her purse. One day she and I had taken the bus to a nearby shopping area, not for heavy every day shopping but more a window shopping expedition. On a back street we went through on our way from the bus to the shops we passed a builders' junk yard and

Mary Datchelor Girls' School, 1931

on the spur of the moment Mum decided to take a look. There she found the perfect window, the right size in a good frame, stained glass and nice looking and best of all, the right price. But - how to get it home? No delivery available and no cars and too big for the bus. We held a consultation and decided we could carry it between us. There was a pathway running along the back streets by the side of the railway lines and if we followed that we would avoid the heavy street traffic both vehicular and pedestrian. So Mum in the front and myself in the rear we set off. It was a bit more than two miles but not until the last mile did we have a problem and then not because of being tired with the heavy load but I suddenly thought how silly we must look rather like the advertisement of a painter carrying a long ladder so I began to giggle. Mum was cross with me at first and then she saw the funny side of it and she began to giggle too. So suddenly there we were laughing like a couple of fools and too weak with laughter to carry the window. We finally had to put it down, wipe our eyes and sober up for the last stretch. Well finally we made it and when installed the window did look nice and kept the front door area warm and dry.

When school started in the autumn after we had moved in at Beckenham and Mum took me in to register at school with the new address etc. she found to her consternation that the information given her at the LCC was incorrect and I had indeed forfeited my scholarship by moving out of the boundaries of London County. Apparently officialdom was no more reliable then than it is now, it all depends who you talk to at any given time. Mum was in a state of shock as there was no way we could afford to have me go to a higher education school without the scholarship but being Mum she did not sit down and cry about it, she wrote to Dr. Brock requesting an appointment to talk to her about me. The upshot of that meeting was that I was given a private scholarship financed from private grants and bequests and this would replace the public scholarship that I had won.

I now began the routine that I was to follow for the next few years; a twenty minute walk to the railway station, a ten minute trip in one train, change to another line by a short walk over a bridge, another ten minute train ride and then the final lap, another twenty minute walk to school. It was a long way to go but we never thought much about it, only the wealthy had cars and even if we had one it certainly would not have been used to ferry children around when they were perfectly capable of walking. Dad and Doug went their respective ways from the same station but we never went at the same time so did not travel together unless one of us had a change in the normal timetable for one reason or another. I got a season ticket on the railway so on the weekends I was able to travel to see my friends without any additional cost so we kept in touch easily.

My first years at school went well, I was not brilliant but got by with satisfactory marks. It is hard to define my own personal feelings. I was not a popular person, not disliked but often on the outside looking in. I was not pretty - I wore the thick spectacles that brought forth hated nicknames - my parents did not have money nor were they in any social sphere and I was not good at sports so there was no particular clique that I belonged in. I don't mean to say that I was unhappy either, I had my own circle of friends and with time developed some close friendships although only one person out of the many at school actually remained a friend

Mary Datchelor Girls' School, 1931

after school days. I did not really become friendly with Joan until my third year but we remained close until her death in 1978 shortly after she had visited me in California.

Most of my contemporaries when they were fourteen or so went through the "film star craze" and were caught often mooning over a film stars picture or reading film magazines when they should have been studying. At that age I had no interest in such things, I must have matured later than the others, so my work went well and I studied hard. Then, just at the worst possible time for me, when I was about fifteen I caught the "bug" and while my friends were now buckling down I was doing the reverse and my studies began to fall off. This was no time for this to happen as the matriculation exam was just ahead. My teachers scolded me, my parents were worried and cajoled and scolded but it was like water off a duck's back. It is hard to see, looking back, really what caused this change in my study habits, things were the same at home, homework done routinely, no extra treats, no outings or getting together with friends except at weekends or holidays. Whatever the cause, just plain laziness perhaps, though I think there was a deeper reason than that, my work fell off alarmingly and when the exam came up I failed miserably. I had passed easily in English and French, scraped through in math and history and geography but failed badly in the sciences and Latin.

For some reason the results of the exam were given out on a Saturday so although we did not normally go into school on Saturdays we were all asked to attend to get the results. I had asked for permission to go to a movie matinee at a theatre near the school after getting the exam results so the family did not expect me home until later in the afternoon.

A War Bride's Memoirs

When I heard that I had failed I was so stunned that I could not face going home so I went to the movie anyway. I shall never forget that movie, it was "Bolero" with George Raft and Carole Lombard and I sat through it completely numb, not hearing a word and crying soundlessly all afternoon. I was horrified at the turn of events, desperately ashamed to go home, knowing all my friends had passed while I had disgraced my family.

Finally I had to go home, I could not sit there and cry for ever. Mum and Doug were waiting for me, Dad was out at the library. Doug took one look at my face and disappeared and left me with Mum while I dissolved in tears again. There was very little scolding, just a rather sad discussion as to my future, whether I was to return to school in September and try for the exam again next year or whether I should leave school now and start job hunting without benefit of the matric certificate. This was in July and I would be sixteen in September. The school leaving age was fourteen so I could look for work. Nothing was decided that night, that would be something for Mum and Dad to talk over alone so after a silent dinner I went upstairs to once more cry until I fell asleep exhausted.

It was decided that I was to go back to school, repeat the years courses and try the exam again in a years time. I don't think Dad was particularly in favour of this plan as he felt the failure was entirely due to my own laziness and I should stand the consequences but Mum was still firm in her belief that her children should get the best education and good jobs and she felt that I would really buckle down after this setback.

The summer passed by, not a very happy one with this cloud hanging over my head and in September I returned to

Mary Datchelor Girls' School, 1931

school determined to do my very best and get through the exam with flying colours next spring. But I had not reckoned with the other girls and the pecking order at school. My friends, having passed the exam, were all in grades above me, either taking advanced courses for university or taking secretarial courses and I saw little of them. Those girls who had not been close friends did not miss the opportunity to sneer at me and laugh at me because I had failed. My new classmates all knew that I had failed and they too were superior and unfriendly. I was not mature enough to rise above this atmosphere of failure and my days were miserable as I struggled with my studies feeling very much alone. Gradually in self defence I began to act in a flippant manner as though I did not care and the more I tried to convince others that the exam meant nothing to me the more I convinced myself that I would not pass it anyway so why try. At Christmas my marks were just average, enough to pass the exam "with a bit of luck" but certainly not the marks of someone trying hard to succeed. Mum said little but I knew she was bitterly disappointed and I found I could not discuss my problems within the family but at home as at school I built a wall around myself and pretended that I did not care although inside I was desperately unhappy.

Early in the new year, 1937, Dad decided that he had had enough and at this point Mum agreed with him that I should start looking for work and leave school. It was decided that I should take some of the lower grade Civil Service exams and perhaps take higher ones later on and thus get into the better jobs by this method rather than using the matriculation as the entry into the higher grade levels of the Service. The CS exams were not being given until later in the year so we started looking at newspaper advertisements to find a suitable job for the interim period. When an opening appeared suitable Mum would take me out of school and we would go off for an interview. I well remember pointing out what I thought would be a good job as the prospective employer was a turf accountant and accounting was a very good field. Mum and Dad had a chuckle over this and broke the news to me that "turf accountant" was just a fancy name for a bookie. Not a suitable job at all.

I got a job to start with at a jewellers in Hatton Garden, light general office work and mostly, it seemed to me, making tea and running errands for the various men in the office. A very dark dingy hole in the wall office and when I got a call from the employment agency that they had an interview for me for the job of junior clerk at the British Iron & Steel Federation I made up my mind to get it if at all possible. The B.I.S.F. office was a new imposing glass and concrete building that sparkled with cleanliness, it was not too far from a central railway station and the position and pay were better than the one I had now. I went for the interview and happily got the job, a clean start in more ways than one.

The job itself was not marvellous but it was a starting point and with a good company. The woman boss of the department I worked in was a real martinet but in those days humble workers did not expect much consideration and it was good training for me as she expected, and saw that she got, my best efforts and no fooling around. The other women in the office were mostly ten years older than I but on the whole a pleasant group. One of my duties was to pick up mail from the office of the one of the officers of the company and I was intrigued to find that he was married to Ann Todd, the film star and there was a picture of her on his desk. That was the closest I had ever come to a famous person and I found it exciting. At one time when I was helping his secretary she was writing a letter to Fred Perry, the tennis star, to ask him to go to their house to "open" their new tennis court and that seemed very romantic to me.

In May, 1937 came the coronation of King George VI and Queen Elizabeth. The B.I.S.F. offices were down a side street near Westminster Abbey and the entrance to the Abbey could be seen from some of the office windows. All the employees were given tickets that enabled them to get through the street that would be normally closed to other than official personnel and permit them to come into the office. Victor Halcolm, the director married to Ann Todd, very kindly gave me a couple of extra tickets so that my whole family could come and rather to my surprise even my Dad was excited at the idea. We knew we would not be able to see the actual procession but these streets adjacent to the Abbey would be filled with much excitement and we would be able to hear the bands and the hustle and bustle if nothing else.

Dad carefully worked out how we would get there and how early we would have to start as the street would be closed even to ticket holders after a certain time. We also knew that busses and tubes would be packed so we had to allow plenty of time. Dad put in an alarm call on the phone and when the great day dawned we were up and on our way soon after four in the morning. We took the train up to town and then the tube from Charing Cross the same way that I travelled to work every day. Our passes were checked by police at the street corner and we went into the office and took our seats at one of the windows watching for any signs of activity at the Abbey and constantly intrigued by the people passing below us in the street. By nine o'clock the street was closed off and we heard over the radio that the procession had left Buckingham Palace for the Abbey. We could hear music in the distance and the roar of the crowds also distantly.

The big excitement came when we found that our street was one of those chosen to accommodate various military groups who had escorted the King and Queen to the Abbey and now had to wait while the service took place. They would be having their lunch and grooming their horses ready for the return to the Palace. We ourselves had brought packed lunches with us with the company providing cups of tea and after we had eaten one of my friends and I went down to talk to the soldiers and give sugar to the horses. We also collected autographs as souvenirs of the big day. There was a contingent of the Royal Canadian Mounted Police, a group of New Zealanders and two Indian regiments in full dress uniform with brilliant coloured turbans. The horses were beautiful animals and of course all the accoutrements were polished to the nth. degree. We spent a fascinating hour and then the police asked us to return to our seats as the troops had to get ready to leave. Very soon they mounted up and we watched as they rode away towards the Abbey.

We craned our heads and swore that we caught a glimpse of the little princesses standing outside the Abbey for just a moment. Then the cheering and the music died away and we knew that the procession had left this area. Now it was time to leave and we thought it would be a quiet walk to the tube and a quiet journey home. What a mistake that was! We

Mary Datchelor Girls' School, 1931

walked towards the Abbey and the streets were ankle deep in newspapers. Thousands of people had been waiting in the streets all night and covered themselves with newspapers for warmth after reading the paper last night or this morning. It had begun to rain lightly and much of the paper was wet and swirled around our feet in a soggy mess. The street cleaners could not tackle it until people moved out of the way and the people could not move very quickly.

    Dad gathered us all together and made sure that we did not get separated from each other in the masses of people. It was a unique experience. In front of the Abbey there were some peers who apparently got stuck there as their limousines could not get through the crowds to pick them up. As soon as the procession had departed all the crowds broke up into little groups of jollification and good cheer and wandered all over the road with absolutely no regard for any motor traffic, after all they outnumbered the cars by a hundred to one for once. So here we saw people in court dress hitching up their robes and walking with the rest of us trying to get to the tube. When we finally did get on the tube I found myself strap hanging next to a woman in a long dress with an ermine edged cloak over her arm and wearing a coronet topped with the court head-dress of three white feathers. What a day - I can still feel the excitement of the crowds.

    A few months after this I was notified that I had passed the Civil Service exam I had taken earlier and although I was a bit lukewarm about changing jobs again my parents were anxious that I should take up the Civil Service post as it had better prospects for the future. I accepted the post and in a few weeks after the necessary physical exams and interviews I left the B.I.S.F. and started my new career as a clerical assistant in the HQ of the London Telephone Service. I had promised Mum that I would study and take higher exams within the Service but meanwhile I had a lot to learn on my new job.

I have talked a lot about the jobs etc. but not much about my free time. Some of my closest friends were still in school and others just beginning jobs like myself. None of us had much free time and certainly very little money for amusement. We enjoyed getting together in each others homes, we went to the cinema fairly often and we went up to town to go to the theatre, opera and ballet and to symphony concerts. My starting salary in the C.S. was 17/6 a week (about $3.50 at the 1938 rate of exchange) and of course out of that I had to contribute to my upkeep at home. I would usually also take Mum a "little something" every pay day, a few chocolates or a peach. Yes, "a" peach as the only ones available at that time were hot house grown and very expensive - never thought I would live to see the day when they could be bought by the pound.

A seat in the "Gods", the highest and cheapest balcony seat for the Sadler's Wells ballet or for the Covent Garden Opera was about sixpence (about a dime) and we got last minute theatre tickets at half price also very cheaply. Sometimes my best friend, Joan, would come over to my office at the end of the day and we would have a meal in a teashop and then go ice skating. Well actually we never did much skating but we would waddle around on the ice trying to skate and having loads of fun. On the weekend we might meet and go to the zoo or just go shopping enjoying each others company. It was a very simple unsophisticated life but

Mary Datchelor Girls' School, 1931

we enjoyed it and we never had any worries about coming home late at night alone on the train or bus or walking through streets to our home from the station. Of course there was crime but it was very rare for it to touch the innocent in quiet residential neighbourhoods.

Spectre of War, 1938

In late summer of 1938 Hitler's claims in Europe became more violent and his territorial demands focused on Czechoslovakia. Chamberlain, the Prime Minister, flew back and forth to Germany and in the London parks trenches were dug and air raid shelters begun. All civilians were issued with gas masks that came in neat little cardboard boxes with a long string attached so that they could be carried hanging from our shoulders. Mum and Dad went around looking rather grim, Mum's brother was still a semi invalid from gas in the last war, and Dad had very vivid memories of warfare, but to us young ones it did not mean very much. In September Chamberlain came back from Munich and made his famous "Peace in our time" speech and we all breathed a sigh of relief and stuffed the gas masks in the back of a cupboard. Actually we did not realise, at least I should say "I" did not realise all that had transpired. Chamberlain had caved in to Hitler, the country's honour was at a low ebb but in retrospect although he did not do it with this in mind perhaps he did the best thing. It gave us a year to build up our defences a little and develop some kind of military strength. Far from what was eventually needed but at least the beginnings. We had betrayed Czechoslovakia but we were in no position to help her at this time.

Meanwhile I was adjusting to work in the Civil Service. At first I missed the bright clean surroundings of the new B.I.S.F. building. His Majesty's Government has never been noted for beautiful buildings for their workers and the L.T.S.

Spectre of War, 1938

was housed in Cromwell House, a rather dark, dingy building at the end of Waterloo Bridge, a few blocks from the Old Vic Theatre. I remember one lunch time I was excited to pass in the street the star, Robert Donat, who had apparently just come from rehearsal at the Old Vic where he was appearing.

My supervisor, a middle aged woman, was very pleasant and helpful and obviously used to taking in green workers and setting them on the right path. She did this with more tact and camaraderie than the manager I had had at the B.I.S.F. My co-workers were quite a friendly crowd too, one a little over friendly in a way that vaguely embarrassed me. One day I heard one of the other women tell the extra friendly one to "Layoff that kid" and she did leave me alone for a while. Such was my innocence then (imagine a 19 year old today!) that it was years before I realised looking back that the "friendly" one was probably what we today would call "gay".

I must recount a terrible mistake I made in those early weeks. Very funny looking back on it but not funny then, in fact quite a serious goof. In those days before automation in the telephones there were paper tickets prepared for all calls made from a telephone box through an operator. These pieces of flimsy paper were about 1,1/2 x 2,1/2 and came in to us from the telephone exchanges packed tightly together and tied into bundles. In fact the supervisor would measure the length of a bundle to ascertain how much work was involved in processing them. The tickets were either left blank or would have a 2, 3 or 4 written on them indicating either the minimum charge, one penny, or two pence, three pence etc. We had to count all those flimsies adding as we went and when we reached a pound (240 pence) they were rubber banded in stacks. The girl who was training me told me just to count the tickets with figures on and toss the blank ones away. She did not explain that the blank ones were worth a penny and would be counted separately later so I took her literally and all day long tossed them away - right into the waste paper basket. Late in the afternoon the supervisor came around to collect the blanks to be counted and my "slight" error was discovered, also the fact that the porters had already been around and emptied the waste paper baskets!

To do Miss Johnson credit, she did not have hysterics or kill me but she and I went down to the depths of the building where all the rubbish was awaiting disposal and we waded through mountains of paper and string picking out a bundle of tickets here and an odd ticket or two there. I was sure that would be the end of my promising career but the importance of the tickets was explained to me and that was the end of the affair.

I took the promotional exam in the Spring of 1939 and passed every subject with ease except for math, missing that by only a couple of points. I knew what had done it too. There was a geometry question, using a simple formula but requiring a drawing of a door ajar and I had panicked knowing how hard I found those drawings to do, tried to explain the theorem without the diagram and had completely messed up that question. I was really disappointed and my parents felt badly for me too for I had worked hard the past few months. It was decided that I should have some individual tutoring in math and try for the exam again in early September. I took a month off for a bit of relaxing (after office hours of course) and then started being coached two evenings a week with a math tutor.

Spectre of War, 1938

Meanwhile a troubled Europe was preparing for the inevitable. It had been a very uneasy year since Munich and as the year progressed more danger signals appeared. I was too wrapped up in my own affairs to think much about it and truth to tell the thought of a war was rather exciting, something that might pep up my life. In August more air raid shelters began to appear and we were told to get out those gas masks and dust them off. Barrage balloons appeared for the first time in London skies and there was talk about government offices being sent out of the city.

Then one eventful evening just before I was to go to my math lesson there was an announcement on the radio during the news saying that due to the political crisis and uncertain future all scheduled Civil Service exams had been cancelled until further notice. What a blow - all my studying and Dad's hard cash for the lessons was now wasted. Well there was nothing we could do except hope the crisis would not last long and the exams would be re-scheduled before I forgot all that my painful cramming had got into my brain. Little did we realise that the "crisis" would not be over for six years and by then who would care about a C.S. exam.

The war clouds came closer and it soon became obvious that we could not avoid the inevitable. It was anticipated that London would be an immediate target for bombing and they began to evacuate children from the city. Mum volunteered to go as an escort with one group of children going into the country and on Sunday morning, September 3rd., she left early for the assembly point. During the day we heard the official announcement that we were now at war. The news was prefaced by the simple statement "This is London", the three words that throughout the next six years would identify news bulletins and any announcements of particular importance on the radio. Although I was young enough to feel excitement rather than fear nevertheless the cold brief statement of the declaration of war gave me a funny feeling in the pit of my stomach. Later that day watching for Mum to return we saw her walking along the railway platform that ran above and parallel to our back garden. She raised her hand in a drinking gesture and by the time she had got to the house her cup of tea was ready and she sat down and told us about her day. And so for us the war began.

As I have said it was expected that London would immediately be subject to heavy bombing but that did not happen and we entered into the phase later called the "phony war". We got used to carrying our gas masks with us always, seeing the sky above filled with barrage balloons and stumbling around in the black out. This was a real trial to everyone, not a chink of light could be shown around a window, all the windows had to have heavy black curtains made unless the current drapes were already completely light proof and very few were. We also had to be sure that we did not open the front door without turning the lights off inside the house and of course never to switch on a light without making sure that the windows were covered. Cars had to have their headlights hooded and the streets after dark became shrouded mysterious places. At first we used to love moonlight nights when we could see where we were going but of course later on we learned to dread the nights with a full moon - a "bomber's moon".

Bath, 1939

A few weeks later my personal life got a jolt. I was told that I was being transferred from the London Telephone Service to the Admiralty as with the rapid expansion of the navy they needed a great deal of clerical help. The next week I was told that the Admiralty except for a few key departments was being moved out of London and I was to report to the city of Bath in western England and go to work there. I think Mum was a bit upset to have her fledgling thrown out of the nest with such short notice but she took it in stride, began washing, ironing, mending etc. and helping me decide what I was to take with me. We were going to be billeted in various private homes scattered throughout the city and in a very few days we were issued with our travel warrants, told where to report and given identity tags to wear, much as we had seen in pictures of refugee camps.

So on a rather damp, depressing day I made my way up to London and to Paddington station for the Bath train, a route I was to get very familiar with in the next few years. We really all thought that this would be more like a few weeks - or at the outside a few months - vacation and looked forward to an early return. I did not see anyone I knew on the train though many people wore similar identity tags. The staffing for the new departments was made up of people from many less important government departments and not too many had been transferred from the L.T.S.

The journey to Bath was about 2,1/2 hours long and so we arrived in early afternoon. There were billeting officers awaiting us and we were gathered in groups going to the same part of the city, loaded into cars with our luggage (limited to one large or two small suitcases) and off we went. We stopped here and there dropping off people and finally I was the only one left in the car. As it turned out I had the billet the farthest away from the office, in fact I was outside the city itself in a small village called Weston.

The people on whom I was billeted were a middle aged couple, well actually a middle aged woman and her husband quite a bit older and retired. They had been expecting Miss Avis to be a much older person and were somewhat surprised when a "young chit of a girl" turned up. The house was in a modern subdivision, the standard three bedroom, one bathroom home, dining room, living room, kitchen and a pleasant garden both back and front of the house. The snag was in the distance from where I was to be working. The bus service, a rural route, was limited at best.

My billetors, Syd and Rose Rowse (though of course we never got past the Mr & Mrs titles although they did call me by my first name) were very pleasant and comparing notes with co-workers later I realised that I was lucky to be in a modern home with a good cook into the bargain. For the fee paid by the government (a chunk of which came out of my salary) the billetor was supposed to provide a bed and breakfast but it was up to the individual employee to find and pay for lunch and dinner either by eating these meals in restaurants or by coming to some financial arrangement with the billetor.

That first evening Mr & Mrs Rowse did their best to make me feel at home and they had a nice dinner ready for me. When they found out where I would be working they

Bath, 1939

were a bit apprehensive as it was a long way from them. They got out bus timetables and found that I could catch one bus into town and then change and catch another from there to my destination. Mrs Rowse suggested that she pack a lunch for me that first day as I had no idea what eating facilities would be available at work. As it turned out there were none and nothing within literally a mile or so. She also suggested that I eat dinner with them tomorrow and then we could discuss some arrangement after that.

These suggestions sounded good to me. It had been a long hard day and I had no idea what tomorrow would bring so I was glad to soak in a tub and then fall into bed fairly early. I did not sleep too well, rather apprehensive about the morning and truth to tell missing Dad and Mum to talk to, it was after all my first time away from home and they had been left in what we still thought as of as a very likely danger zone.

As in most things reality was much easier than the imagined events. I walked the quarter of a mile to the bus terminus in the village and took the bus into town and there I found many familiar faces waiting to catch the other bus to the office. The office was in fact a girls boarding school, Kingswood, commandeered by the Government, a rambling building high on the top of a hill and, as we found later in the year, the coldest, draughtiest place imaginable.

My department had been set up in what had been a dormitory, the desks set up in two rows the length of the room just as the beds had been, and between each desk was a small wooden divider that had presumably been set up for some privacy between beds. Our files and equipment had been sent down from London and that first morning we spent unpacking boxes and setting up our desks. There were no phones at all and later on when they became available we still only had a couple in the entire room. The room was equipped to hold about twenty people but we had only five or six at the beginning. As time went on and the navy expanded we hired more and more people which to us "professionals" was a bit of a mixed blessing. As Civil Service exams had been suspended we hired temporary people with scant regard for their qualifications as labour was in short supply now and got worse as the war progressed. The "locals" in many cases came direct from factories being closed down or converted to war uses, I remember well the influx of people from a jam factory closed due to lack of sugar, they may have been top notch jam makers but their clerical skills were nil. To add to these we had a lot of local "gentry", women who had never worked but were now compelled by government order to find work unless they had young children in the household. Many of these became excellent employees but at first chafed under restrictions and had a hard time accepting discipline, especially if the supervisor was younger than they were. Of course this was all a gradual process over the next couple of years, I am getting a bit ahead of myself.

  I began to settle down into a routine, the bus trip was long but the connections were not bad. I came to an arrangement with Mrs Rowse and she provided me with lunches to take to work and dinner when I got home at night. By the time I paid her and the bus fare and with the billet money taken out of my pay cheque I had very little left to call my own each pay day but there was enough for a movie at the weekends and an occasional meal out with friends.

  That first winter of the war was marked largely by boredom and frustration. There was as yet no sense of

Bath, 1939

urgency or fear. There had been scattered incidents, ships had been lost to U-boats and the R.A.F. had bombed German boats in their harbours and in December came the exciting sea chase ending with the scuttling of the German boat the Graf Spee by its commander, but all this was rather remote and unreal to us on the home front. Poland was lost, the German alliance with Russia was announced and Finland attacked by Russia but western Europe was still relatively untouched. At home we were mostly affected by gradually increasing shortages of various items. Food became a big topic of conversation although rationing at this time was not stringent. Things like oranges and bananas had disappeared completely. I remember a little girl born next door to us in London the first week of the war looking in amazement at a banana given to her on her sixth birthday and wondering why she could not eat the skin as she did with an apple. Meat and dairy products were also starting to become harder to get although we had not arrived yet at the meat ration of 1/- (about 25 cents) a week or the one egg a month standard. We were all enrolled in Air Raid Precaution (ARP) groups although at this point it was not compulsory and although conscription was in force for men it was a gradual process and there were still plenty of young men at the office.

Then suddenly in the spring of 1940 Denmark and Norway were invaded followed quickly by Belgium and Holland and then before we had adjusted to this news France was invaded, the famous Maginot Line was found to be useless and we were faced with the British defeat and retreat at Dunkirk. The whole complexion of our lives was changed, no longer were we onlookers but participants and the war was on our very doorstep. Now ARP took on new dimensions, we were expecting invasion also and overnight the fields around us were studded with huge concrete blocks for tank traps. On one occasion a German reconnaissance plane slipped through the area's limited defences and came down low over the office and we saw it clearly. Then distant anti-aircraft fire could be heard and the plane rose into the clouds and disappeared.

Another aspect of security was that the building now was patrolled by navy guards and we were issued with passes that had to be shown before we could enter the building. I well remember one incident on ARP night duty later that year. Six of us "had the duty" that night. We slept in a small building separate from the office wing and in pairs we would patrol the office and other buildings for a two hour stretch and then sleep for four hours. My partner at that time was Kay Stoneham, a very interesting person. She was much older than I and had lived most of her life in Kenya, she joked that the equator ran right through her kitchen. Her husband was a well known author and when at the beginning of the war they left Kenya they had lived at first in an artists colony in Devon. The peaceful atmosphere of that place had gone by 1940 and they had moved to Bath "for the duration" to use the phrase on everyone's lips.

This particular night we had the 3am to 5am patrol shift. We had one tin hat and one flashlight between us - who would get the tin hat in case of dire need was questionable but I had an uneasy feeling that Kay's 5ft.6 would over come my 5ft.1 very easily. We patrolled the entire school and as we were going up a narrow winding staircase to the top of the clock tower we heard the sound of a Messerschmitt plane with its distinctive staccato engine. Our orders were in such a situation to immediately arouse all the other fire watchers so

Bath, 1939

with one accord, partly due to "orders" and partly due to sheer fright we dashed down the stairs, Kay running for one exit and myself to the other. I ran around the corner of the building and suddenly out of the gloom came a figure and a bayonet six inches from my stomach. I stopped dead, my heart pounding and identified myself to the sentry. He was as jittery as I and gave me a lecture - in very ripe naval language - on the danger of wearing rubber soled shoes and creeping up on an armed sentry. Most of our naval guards were men who had been torpedoed and were given this easy shore job as a temporary rest assignment before going back to sea so many of them were in a nervous state to begin with. By the time I caught up with Kay and we roused the rest of the group the enemy plane had long since gone and it was an "all quiet" situation then until daylight.

In August the concentrated bombing of London, the "blitz" had begun but in spite of this I was determined to go home for my 20th. birthday in September. My brother who had been conscripted a few months ago had 48 hours leave at the same time so we would all be together for the weekend.

I took the Friday off and took the train up to London getting home just after lunch and coinciding perfectly with one of the first daylight raids on the London dock area. Dad was out on air raid duty so Mum and I headed for the Anderson. The "Anderson" named after the government minister who came up with the idea was a small one family air raid shelter at the end of our garden. They had been issued to all families requesting one in the past few months. It had steel sides and a roof and was sunk in the ground about two feet. There was just enough room for four or five people to gather and before long we had ours equipped with a couple of chairs, some food supplies and water and some magazines. We also had a flashlight in case of emergency but of course due to the black out we could not use it unless the doorway was blocked off so its use was limited.

It was my first experience of an air raid and it was not close enough to be too terrifying, much of the noise coming from our own anti aircraft guns. Late in the afternoon the all clear sounded and when Dad came home he said that they needed people at the local school to help with the influx of refugees arriving from the bombed out dock areas. I grabbed a quick sandwich and walked down to the nearest school where I helped in setting up army cots etc. in the halls and corridors. We were told that this school was a secondary centre as it was quite a long way from the damaged area and if no evacuees arrived within the next couple of hours we could go home.

A great idea but within an hour it was dark and in the darkness came the bombers, great waves of them coming in much closer to us than the afternoon raid had done. We were debating whether to go outside and make a dash for home when some ARP men came in and said it was much too dangerous. They decided that where we were waiting was not too safe either with the big plate glass windows so we made our way down to the school basement and huddled together in the coal cellar. Eventually at dawn came the all clear and I left the others and walked through the empty streets looking at the scarlet sky above, evidence of the enormous fires burning by the river.

Mum was anxiously awaiting me although she knew from Dad that I was spending the night at the school. By the time I had breakfasted and cleaned up Doug had arrived but our

Bath, 1939

peace was short-lived. The next two days we spent in and out of the shelter the whole time. There barely seemed time between raids to get a bite to eat and to go to the bathroom. The ack-ack guns were now being run up and down the railway lines near the house and the noise of those going off a couple of hundred yards from our shelter was more nerve wracking than anything. At one point on Sunday afternoon Doug got bored with the confinement and said he was going to take a walk as things seemed to have quieted down a bit. As he started out he called Mum and I to come and look at the sky. There were a couple of dozen planes flying in formation clearly seen in the sunshine and Mum and I puffed up with pride at our great R.A.F. - until Doug pointed out that the R.A.F. on defensive does not fly in formation and those were masses of German bombers we were looking at! As we looked we did see one lone plane go in and tackle a formation and the group broke up and the fighter picked out one bomber and herded it to the ground. We could not hear the plane's gun fire but we saw the bomber's crew parachute out and heard the explosion when the bomber hit the ground. We cheered as at a football match. One down! But how many hundreds to go.

Doug and I had to leave the next day, both of us heading to places of safety but leaving Mum and Dad in the thick of it. Every night now the attacks came in different parts of London. Dad was on duty most nights after work and Mum was alone in the Anderson. They moved a mattress into the shelter so that Mum could at least lay down and Mum had thermoses of tea so that if there was a quiet spell Dad could stop off, get a cup of tea and make sure Mum was safe. There came a night when Dad's partner was killed. They had been together all night, the all clear had not yet sounded but it had been quiet for a while and it was almost daylight. Dad said he thought he would go home and shower and shave ready for work in the morning and his partner said he would take one more turn around the block and then head for home too but he never made it. A lone bomber jettisoning the last of his load on the way home came over by the park. Dad, almost at our front door, threw himself on the ground and was safe. His partner, a hundred yards away, was killed by the blast. No houses were damaged but a couple of Andersons were. Luckily the people who had been in there earlier had gone into their houses during the lull.

After this close shave Dad had an uneasy feeling about the Anderson and finally called me and asked if I could find somewhere for Mum to come and stay for a few weeks, he wanted her out of the raids for a while. He must have been psychic as just before she returned home some weeks later the Anderson was badly damaged by a blast, one side blown out and Mum would certainly have been killed if she had been there.

It did not make sense for Mum and I not to be together in Bath so I found some rooms for the two of us and left my billet in Weston. It worked out pretty well for a couple of months but Mum was anxious to get back to her home and be with the other Londoners, not "hiding in the country" as she said. The raids had lessened somewhat and Dad too was anxious to have her home so off she went and I was alone again.

I decided not to go back to my billet. Mrs Rowse said I would be very welcome but the house was so far out of town that I could not have any social life, the last bus for the village

Bath, 1939

leaving town by nine in the evening. So I checked around and found a place right in the centre of town. Strictly speaking it was not a billet but a boarding house but with the lack of casual boarders the owner of the house was more than willing to take in billettees and collect the government money. There were eight of us women there, three girls who worked in various city places and rented rooms and five of us Civil Servants. It was a very friendly group and I was much happier in the swim of things rather than spending every evening with an older couple however nice they were.

Life took on a more hectic, exciting tone. All of us in the CS worked a minimum of a 54 hour week plus Saturday and Sunday duty when required. We also had regular fire warden duties at various places in the city but we still had time for fun. I took up riding lessons and became one of the officers of the Admiralty Riding Club. I was never much good at riding but I enjoyed it - except when I got a horse who knew he had a rank rookie on his back and acted up accordingly. I was cantering across some fields with some friends one time and we passed a group of Canadian soldiers walking along the footpath. One of them pulled off his cap and waved it in the air, yelling "Ride 'em Cowboy" at the top of his lungs. My horse promptly took fright, reared up and deposited me on the ground. I was unhurt but mortified. Sure made the Canadian's day though, he laughed all the way back to camp.

In late 1940 I had two letters that cheered me up. I had written to my friends in Denmark and Norway through the Red Cross, not really letters but a few sentences on a pre-printed form that the Red Cross provided. I had answers to both of my notes. This was the only letter I had from Inge in Copenhagen until after the war but I had two more notes from Sigrid in Norway. However I never did get to meet my pen pal, Sigrid. After the war when I wrote to her I had a short note from her parents telling me that she had been killed working for the underground, no details and I never heard from them again.

1941 brought Germany's attack on Russia and there was some lessening of the air attacks on England, at least on London. On the lighter side there was also a side benefit for one of our number. One of our supervisors was an older bachelor, Charlie Reeves. If it had not been for the war he would have been retired by now, his health was not too good and he was very deaf, but a charming, friendly man. By sheer bad luck he had been billeted on a retired military man who ran his home as he would have done an army camp. From the beginning of the war the major news broadcast in the evening was preceded by the playing of the national anthems of the allies and as the war progressed and the number of allies increased so did the length of time the performance took. The military man demanded that his billettees not only listened to the anthems but that they stand at attention throughout. Charlie, being an amiable sort went along with this but due to his deafness never stood up at the right moment and was constantly having to be nudged by one of the others or risk an angry comment from the military. The day after Germany attacked Russia Charlie came in to work with a big grin, it seemed that his host could not contemplate standing to attention for the playing of the Russian national anthem so he decreed that the radio would not be turned on until after the anthems. Now Charlie could sit and enjoy the news without the military preliminaries.

Bath, 1939

1941 was also a year for weddings amongst my friends and I was able to attend some of those in London combining a quick trip home with the festivities. The wedding I attended in Wales during March that year had an unexpected twist. Compulsory conscription for women had been ordered and the day of the wedding was also the day for the first group of women to register. I fell into the first group and so did some other women attending the wedding so after the ceremony the bride's father took a group of us to the registration centre. The bride herself did not have to register on that day, rather a pity as she could have brightened up the proceedings if she had attended in her wedding dress. I say wedding dress because at that time clothes rationing was not too strict and it was still possible to have the traditional white gown. The groom of course was in uniform.

Our office was expanding rapidly, I worked in Dependants' Allowances Branch, figuring and issuing allowances for the dependants of navy ratings and as the navy enlarged so did our work. Amongst the allowances awarded to prevent hardship (and more important to prevent loss of morale in the navy) was one called the UDLAW allowance, that is for an unmarried dependant living as a wife. To qualify for this there had to be proof that the woman and the rating had lived together as husband and wife for a specified time prior to his entry into the navy, or prior to the war if he was a regular and not a conscript. Talk about sailors with a wife in every port - it was amazing the things we turned up and in some cases the man did in fact have two "wives" who qualified. Came the day that the Archbishop of Canterbury got to know of this and blasted the government for encouraging such goings on. His comments hit the papers of course and some wag promptly christened the women in these cases as "Canterbury Belles" (after the flower Canterbury Bell that was in blossom everywhere just about the time that this hit the press) and from then on, except in the most official documents, the UDLAW programme became the CB programme. Anyway whether with CBs or with other types of dependants we were very busy.

To add to the fun about this time down from the top brass came an A.F.O. (Admiralty Fleet Order) that we should be prepared to continue working under a gas attack so once a week we had to don our gas masks and work in them for an hour. Of course the Powers that Be ignored the fact that it was impossible to wear glasses under a civilian type mask and we were not issued with this military type so I for one spent an hour once a week doing nothing but sitting there making snorting and snuffling noises. Couldn't see a thing without my glasses.

As the department enlarged it became obvious that we could not continue to work in the confines of the school so the Navy took over a large area of vacant land on the outskirts of town and hastily built "hutments", one story thrown together buildings, military type. With military help they went up quickly and late in 1941 our offices, together with several other departments moved in. Most of the hotels in the city were occupied by other Admiralty departments and these continued to be used with the overflow going to the huts. The new location was quite a bus ride out of town but I enjoyed the billet I was in so I decided to stay there. I had made friends and we enjoyed ourselves. Two of the non Civil Service girls had been drafted, one into the air force and one into the army where she eventually became a sergeant in an

Bath, 1939

anti aircraft battery that had several German planes to their credit. I and some of my friends volunteered for the services but were turned down as the work we were doing was classified as necessary to the war effort. Maybe it was but I did not feel as if I was doing much.

Doug, too, was out of the army. There was such a shortage of teachers that all teachers were released from the army unless they were on some very highly specialised assignment. He was not very happy about it, glad to get back to teaching and rid of some of the army hardships, but he felt a bit of a slacker back as a civilian.

At the end of the year America was pulled into the war by the attack on Pearl Harbour on December 7th. and the day afterwards Malaya was attacked and two British warships were sunk. This meant something to us personally as the captain of the Prince of Wales had been in the Naval Ordnance department in Bath until being appointed to the ship. Hylda, one of my friends, had been his secretary and we grieved with her when he went down with the ship.

Heavier London raids began again as did raids on south coast cities and on northern industrial centres. Although we were in a "safe" city the people at the top were a bit nervous. After all the city was ringed with airfields and the Germans were not exactly known for sticking to military targets anyway. It was decided that all important records should be copied with one set sent away for safe keeping and so we all went to work on overtime laboriously copying paper after paper. All done by hand as copying then was a bit primitive anyway and we had scant facilities as the military came first. I tell this story as it had a funny ending, typical but funny. We worked day and night and finally everything was done, all the copies packed up and trucked away to some lonely storage shack deep in the woods and miles away from any town. Two days after the job was completed a lone Jerry bomber heading for home jettisoned its last bomb at random and - you've guessed it - hit the storage shack fair and square! So much for that great idea.

In April 1942 the Baedeker raids began, so named because they were deliberately aimed not at military targets but at historic places that had figured in the famous Baedeker tourist guides before the war. The first place to be attacked was Exeter where the cathedral dating from 1107 was a target and then came Bath's turn. We had had an occasional raid but mostly these had been concentrated on the port of Bristol about twenty miles away with Bath just being on the receiving end of a left over bomb or two as the raiders hurried for home. But now for two terrifying nights we became the targets of saturation attacks.

The first night we spent most of the night in the basement of the house huddling together in semi darkness listening to the whistle of the bombs, some muted anti aircraft fire and the clanging of fire engine bells. Just before dawn there came such a loud scream of a bomb that involuntarily we all crouched closer to the floor staring bleakly into each others eyes. There was no sound of a bomb exploding just a sort of thump and a tremor in the ground. A few moments later at the same time as the "all clear" sounded we heard fire engines dashing past the house and screeching to a stop. We hurried up the stairs to look out on the night's damage. Flames were pouring from the basement of a house a few doors away and just beyond that was a gaping hole in the ground where two houses had stood. By a stroke of

Bath, 1939

remarkable fortune both destroyed houses had been empty at the time they were hit but in the fire in the adjacent house three women died. One, a doctor, had been out all night helping wherever she could and in the lull just before the raid ended she had told the people she was working with that she would quickly check on her mother and aunt and would be right back. In just the moment that she returned to her house the bomb struck and started the incredible blaze and she and the others died in the flames.

In the morning came the realisation that many parts of the city were very badly damaged and at work some faces were missing, co-workers killed. From the German propaganda radio came the message that tonight Bath would be obliterated so my friends and I decided that we would not wait like rats caught in a trap in the basement again so we decided to go up on the hills and soon after dusk we walked a few miles and huddled in the hedgerows. It was scarcely less terrifying the steady drone of the planes and the scream of the bombs was louder in the open air and the crack of the ack-ack shells was also frightening. The night seemed endless and then as dawn came a new terror was added. German planes having dropped their bombs began machine gunning along the hedgerows and in the open fields where people had gathered. Fortunately it was not a heavy attack, more in the nature of a parting shot and the casualties were light. Didn't do a thing for my morale, though and I was never so glad to see full daylight and the sound of the "all clear" was the sweetest music. These two night raids were the only ones directly aimed at Bath, the following nights the cities of York and Norwich were similarly attacked. The two raids on Bath left 19,000 buildings destroyed, 400 people killed and 800 seriously injured.

Later that year I and everyone else was served notice by the city that fire watching was now compulsory and would no longer be on strictly a volunteer basis. This did not make much difference to me as I had been fire watching for months anyway but it did mean that I now had to take a brief course, had an identification card issued by the city and could no longer beg off duty just by getting a friend to replace me.

In addition to these air raid duties I had joined the Women's Auxiliary Home Guard attached to the 6th Battalion of the Somerset Light Infantry. There were not enough uniforms to go around so the men got the uniforms and we were issued with such things as a plastic badge, a service type gas mask (now I could wear glasses!) and a certificate stating that if I was captured even though I was not in uniform I was entitled to be treated as a member of the armed forces with the rank of private – big deal!

One of the first things on the agenda as a H.G. Pte. was to go through a gas test, as based on the use in World War I we still expected to be subjected to gas attacks if an invasion started. We went in groups of about a dozen and after a short lecture by an officer – regular army type not Home Guard – went into a small one room building where we were told to put on our gas masks. The building was then filled with some kind of gas and we stood there for a short time wheezing in and out while the officer finished his lecture on the various types of gas and told us that as we were feeling no effects then it showed how good the gas masks were. Then to finally rub the point home we were told to take off our masks and

Bath, 1939

we had to breathe the stuff until our eyes ran and we were all coughing and choking. He had proved his point.

A couple of incidents with the Home Guard bear mentioning although they both happened about a year later. One time I was on evening duty and had been told that at 9pm I would be relieved by a regular army officer, a certain Captain Chapman. Also during the course of the evening I would be getting some messages brought in by dispatch riders, regular army and I should hold these for the Captain. The Home Guard HQ for the area was in a five storey hundred year old house completely empty except for a few things on the ground floor, a switchboard, table and chair and cot. With blackout screens up at all the windows that rattled with every breath of air and with the usual creaks and groans from a large empty house it was a spooky place to spend several hours alone. But there I sat on the hard chair and tried to convince myself that I really was doing something important for King and Country. Each time the switchboard buzzed I jumped a foot in the air and I was glad when the dispatch riders came in although they stayed only a moment each time before hopping back on their motor bikes and roaring off into the dark.

Nine o'clock came and went but I had to stay on duty until relieved and finally about eleven in came a smartly uniformed officer. He looked a little taken aback at seeing me, no doubt when he heard he was to take over from a Home Guard type he had expected a uniformed male not a scared looking female in casual slacks and sweater. I followed orders and just in case he turned out to be a German spy (though no-one had told me what to do if he was!) I asked to see his identification. He produced an ID card and in my nervous state I could not focus on it at all. The word "black" jumped out at me and in a feeble voice I said I was not expecting a Captain Black but a Captain Chapman - thus of course giving away any code name to the obvious spy. He gave me a supercilious look, jabbed his finger on the ID card pointed to the name "Chapman" (in very small letters) and said that the word "Black" denoted the colour of his hair! So, somewhat ingloriously ended that particular effort on my part to win the war. I have often wondered if he tells that story as often as I do, bet he had a good laugh in the mess the next day.

So with ARP and Home Guard my life was pretty busy. We got railway passes to go home every three months and if we could wangle a Saturday off with no other duties we might dash home for the weekend. The trains ran pretty much on schedule unless there had been a really bad raid, packed of course it was usually standing all the way, but they got us there.

Things were going pretty well at home although on one occasion the house looked different and I could not quite figure out why. Then Dad pointed out that all our ornamental iron railings etc. had gone, requisitioned by the powers that be to help in the metal shortage needed for armaments. There had also been some damage to our roof from one of our own ack-ack shells. The explosion had blown out Mum & Dad's bedroom window and smashed the plate glass mirror on the dressing table. Glass blew everywhere and the pillows on the bed were ripped with slicing jagged pieces of glass. Luckily Mum was not in bed when it happened so the only damage was to the house and no one was injured.

Jake Brown, 1943

I dated and went to dances with other girls. Most of our dates were Americans, no British soldiers to be seen they were all overseas. There were a few Canadian and Australians around and the odd (sometimes very odd!) Dutch, Norwegian and French men but Bath was ringed with airfields the majority of which were those of the U.S. Army. They used to get dances going and would send in army trucks to transport girls to the dances as there was no other means of transportation, public busses out of town stopped running in the late afternoon and of course no ordinary civilian had fuel for cars. At first it seemed odd and rather cheap to climb into an army truck to be transported to a dance but everyone was doing it and it was either that or stay home with our knitting - or rather, no knitting, no yarn. Looking back it seemed we made a lot of dates but also broke a lot of them. Partly this was because few of the dates were firm commitments as neither party knew whether they would be free at any given time, it was more of a "Hope to be in town on Saturday, if you are near the bus stop maybe we can get together" type of thing.

In late 1943 I had met Jake Brown, a sgt. with the 8th. Army Air Corps, at a dance I had gone to with my friend, Pam. Pam was dating quite regularly a soldier who was married and had made it quite plain that he had no intention of cheating on his wife but wanted just friendship to fill the lonely days. Pam went along with this although I personally felt that it was not a good idea as she began to get very fond of Carl and of course he did not reciprocate. Anyway through them I met Jake and whenever he came into town he would give me a call and if I was free we would go out together.

I still have my diary for 1944 and it makes fascinating reading. I had ten days leave at the beginning of the year and I saw the new year in at a dance at an airfield outside Bath, got home about 2am and then packed and got ready for my trip to London that day. My first night in London we had an air raid warning but not too much activity just a lot of gunfire but we did get up and dress and sat around until things quieted down in the early hours of the morning.

I had apparently been saving my clothing coupons as the next day I went on a bit of a shopping spree and bought both a blouse and a dress. My diary also noted that I owed Mum both coupons and money and I would be broke until the end of the quarter!

When I got back to Bath after my leave I got busy with several required Home Guard tests. I passed the switchboard and Morse code tests (can't remember a thing to-day except S.O.S.) but flunked musketry, couldn't have hit a Jerry at two paces. I dated two Americans for a while. I remember Ernie Pyle from Erie, Pennsylvania, nice but, as my diary says, rather uneducated, and someone by the name of Janero Carrillo of whom I have no recollection at all. The other girls in the flat were going out with a group of fellows we had had in for a meal on Christmas day but the Friday evening that I was supposed to go with them I had a call from Jake to say he was in town so I decided to go with him instead.

The next day, Saturday, I worked until five then H.G. duty to eight and ARP until eleven so no dates for me that night. And on the next day, big excitement. A cousin of Sylvia's in the Canadian army turned up unexpectedly bringing with him a tin of salmon and some lemons!!! Now Ed was a nice fellow but if truth were told we enjoyed his gifts more than we enjoyed him. We hadn't seen a lemon for five years and salmon for just about as long. Oh what a feast we had the next day - and we made sure no one dropped in on us to share, this was strictly just for us.

The department that Hylda worked in was staffed mostly by Navy men whereas my department was all civilians, mostly middle aged or older and thus exempt from service. Because of the younger group Hylda's department often arranged social events ranging from dances to hockey matches. I remember playing in one hockey match and I could not think why I was playing so badly, the opposing member was running rings around me. Then I found out that he was an all England and Navy player and I did not even make the team at school, no wonder I was lost.

And although there were so many shortages and restrictions we still went to the symphony, to plays and other shows and we still, when we went to dances at better places in town, wore long evening gowns, several years old of course no new ones to be had. Good job the wartime diet stopped us from getting too fat to wear the same old thing. We used to go into Bristol for symphony concerts as well as going locally, a matinee often because of the bus difficulties, and I well remember one time when the 1812 overture was embellished by the 1942 cannon-fire and bombardment. Sometimes in London people left the theatre if the raids got too heavy or too close but most of the time the play went on and most people stayed put to the end of the play. I suppose all part of the "Business as Usual" attitude.

Of course the biggest thing that strikes me now is that thank Heaven I was young and full of energy - this is a typical entry for a Saturday in February, 1944. "Worked until seven then with Pam to meet Paul and Ken. Had a quick meal and then left to go to a dance at the Officers Mess in Devizes. Spent most of the evening with a Colonel Wallis (Chip) a very pleasant chap whom I hope to see this weekend. Home about one in the morning, not very sleepy so wrote to Mum. Glad tomorrow is Sunday so I don't have to be at work until nine."

In late March I had a weeks leave and so did Jake. I met him in London and we took in several shows and I also showed him around a bit as it was his first visit there. I also took him home to meet my parents and he stayed a couple of nights at my house. He also got his baptism of fire there as both nights we had rather light raids. Dad had had an indoor shelter installed after the destruction of the outside one. This one was rather like a large cage, the top and one side, the side against the wall solid steel and the other side and a removable door of steel mesh. We had put an old mattress inside and if things got too bad we crawled inside and slept there. Mum usually stayed in there at night when Dad was out on air raid duty.

Of course it was not all fun and games and dating, the war was not easing up and we had sad news frequently. One of my friends whose wedding I could not attend as I could not get leave, was married on a Saturday and widowed on the Sunday. Her new husband reported back to his base the day after they were married and did not return that night from a bombing raid. Such things were not uncommon as many

Jake Brown, 1943

marriages took place just on a 24 or 48 hour leave and then the couple went their own ways the next day, many times she, the civilian, in more danger than the military person.

Jake had been transferred to another base so he could not get into Bath but in early May I was able to get a weekend off and went to Saffron Walden where he was stationed. Very romantic, he was on base and the only place he could find for me to stay was a youth hostel lodge, four or more to a room and strictly camping out kind of gear. They must have wondered about me, going camping in high heels and city clothes.

So, on a memorable day, May 6, 1944, Jake asked me to marry him - and I said "No". I liked him a lot but I was not at all sure that I wanted to live in America, I just was not sure of my own feelings. He gave me a very beautiful cameo brooch that he had bought in an antique shop. He had brought it along as a substitute engagement ring until we could buy one I would like and when I turned him down he thought I might as well have the brooch anyway. In spite of my refusal we had a very happy weekend together, walking around the country side and eating at little places before he had to return to camp and I went back to the hostel.

The following weekend Jake had leave and turned up in Bath and after two more days in his company I changed my mind and said yes to his second proposal - sort of nervous about the whole thing but I took the plunge.

During the next month we saw very little of each other. Although we did not know it then things were warming up for D-Day, the airfields were very busy and closed off, no leave, from time to time and I had a lot of extra Home Guard duty. Again, although I did not know it, much of my time spent sending out what I thought were stupid practise messages over the RT was actually a plan to jamb the airwaves.

The V-1 rockets were now pestering London and Mum came down to Bath for a few days rest. One morning at work I was called in by the Department Head, the BIG wheel. He looked at me strangely and asked me if I had "anything to do with an American soldier". I told him that I was engaged to one and my heart went down to my boots as I thought something must have happened to Jake. He then said that an American officer wanted to talk to me and that we could use his office. It turned out that a U.S. Army officer was there to interview me to see if I was a fit person to marry one of their men. I was so darn mad at the insult I almost told him to tell Jake that I wouldn't marry him if General Eisenhower himself begged me to but somehow I managed to keep cool and answered the questions. I still have the letter in which it is stated that the U.S. Army thought it would be OK for me to marry Jake and I would not bring shame upon them. If they were interested in keeping their boys out of shame I could suggest a few places they might check out! And I could tell them a few things about their own officers if disgrace was what they were after.

Anyway the wedding was set for July and as with all wartime marriages it was fraught with various problems. First of all the printed permission to marry did not arrive at Jake's base so the day before the wedding he had to hitch a ride on a plane to the HQ to get it. The plane was badly damaged and being flown in for repair with assorted holes in the fuselage. Jake said it was quite an exciting trip - I can imagine. Then on the day he was due to go on leave the base was shut down and all leave cancelled. His commander said that unofficially Jake could go but if he were stopped by MPs then he was officially AWOL. On that happy note Jake left for London.

We had already got a special wedding license and were to be married in the local Registry Office. The Church of England would not marry us as Jake had not been baptised and the Quakers would not marry us because I was not a Quaker. None of Jake's pals could come because of the base closure and practically none of mine came due to the difficulty of travel although one couple did make it - a day late! Doug came up from Southampton and very nearly put an end to everything. He had borrowed a large American flag to put with the Union Jack as a table decoration and had it packed alongside a jar of jam his landlady had sent up to us, a rare treat in those days. A little of the jam had spilt on the flag and as Doug pulled it out of his suitcase he saw the drop of jam and promptly removed it with a little bit of spit. Now we revere what the flag stands for but not the piece of cloth itself as Americans do and so Jake's eyes nearly popped out of his head at the sight of this callous treatment of his flag.

Mum had made a fruit cake, as she said from blackmail and black-market. She had mixed it while sitting in the air raid shelter and cooked it between raids, praying that if the house was blown up the cake would somehow be preserved. So the cake and a few other goodies for a minute wedding breakfast were set out on top of the Morrison air raid shelter.

That night we slept in the shelter, Mum and Pam, my bridesmaid and I on the inside and Dad and Doug and Jake on the outside. Mum made very sure that I was between her and Pam, no monkey business before the wedding in her house! Actually the men were out of the house most of the night, Dad was on air raid duty and Doug went along to keep him company with Jake joining in from time to time.

The next morning just as the Registrar was about to begin the brief ceremony the air raid sounded. He advised us if things got bad to get under the table and he could continue there. The table did look pretty solid but not exactly blast proof but the raid was light and short with the all clear sounding as we were pronounced man and wife. Incidentally the Registry Office was almost destroyed in a raid two nights later and I often wondered if the records of our marriage went up in smoke.

Our train to Cambridge where we would spend the first night of our honeymoon was slow and long, so much of he track blown up that we had to constantly wait for stretches of empty lines to get through. When we got to the hotel we checked in then immediately had to look for a working phone so that Jake could call his base. The hotel phone was out of action and most of the call boxes were damaged as they had had a raid a couple of nights ago. We eventually found a working phone, Jake made the call and the GI on the other end said it was O.K. for now but be sure to call in twice a day as they were still closed and on alert.

The next day we left Cambridge and went to a lovely old country inn, the Pike and Eel at Overcote several miles out of Cambridge and on the River Great Ouse. Luckily the hotel's phone was working so for two happy days we were able to make the calls twice each day without having to wander all over looking for a phone. On the third morning we got the word "Get back now! We may move out later today" so the idyll ended and within an hour we were in Cambridge awaiting trains to take us in opposite directions.

Jake Brown, 1943

The next two months I was very busy at work. Jake phoned when he could (the alert at his base had been called off) and once in a while was able to get in for a quick visit. He was being interviewed for a commission in the Engineers but he was not too keen on the idea as that would almost certainly have meant going back to the States and then a transfer to the far eastern command. Then on September 13. I had a phone call from Mum to tell me that she had had a call from a friend of Jake's with word that he had gone overseas. Jake had been unable to call as they were on their way to France at a moment's notice so he had asked this friend to call and as he could not reach me the friend had called Mum. A footnote to the commission in the Engineers, we found out years later that several friends in Seattle had been contacted by the FBI for information and references on Jake. It was strange that it did not go through though who knows how an army acts.

Back to London, 1944

With Jake no longer in the country I decided that I would apply for a transfer back to London. Things were less difficult now with the threat of invasion gone and the easing up of the massive air raids. I talked to my boss and he was quite optimistic. He thought I was a bit nuts to want to return to London in view of the occasional V-1 and more frequent V-2 attacks but he agreed to submit my request to the higher ups and within a few weeks I was told that my request had been granted. I had of course kept Jake apprised of my plans in my letters and although he was not too keen on my leaving the comparative safety of Bath he knew I wanted to be with my parents.

As soon as I had applied for the transfer I had begun to pack up odds and ends and had taken two trips home with suitcases laden with clothing. Then when the transfer was official I packed up a truckload of stuff and had it sent home. I was not very keen on the work in the department I had been transferred to but I did not have to work much overtime now, I had been "retired" from both the ARP and the Home Guard so I had a lot of free time. Most of my friends were on their own with their husbands in the military somewhere else so we got together a lot and seldom a week went by without a trip to the cinema or to see a play. The V-2s continued and were very scary but they lessened somewhat as time went on. We sort of got used to counting noses each morning at the office to see if anybody had not made it through the night. During the day it was nerve-wracking to

Back to London, 1944

hear the huge explosions and to know that a V-2 had landed somewhere but we never knew whether it had fallen in our neighbourhood or somewhere else. At least with the V-1s you had some knowledge of where they were headed and of course at night you could clearly see the flame from the tail streaking across the sky.

It was later announced that between May and September 1944 a total of about 8,500 V-1s had been dropped at the rate of about a hundred a day with 95% of them in the London area. They had caused about 6,000 deaths 16,000 injured and damaged well over a million homes. I think the closest I had come to one - well not that close but close enough to be frightening – was shortly before Jake and I were married. We were walking across St. James' Park in London and we heard the noise of a V-1. We looked up and saw it in the sky directly above us and just then the motor cut out. Most of the V-1s dropped like a stone when the motor stopped but some glided for a while travelling a mile or so before crashing. We started to dive for a nearby shelter but then realised that this was one of the new type that would drift so we were safe while it continued on to crash farther away, and in a few moments we heard the explosion.

I wrote to Jake every day and had letters from him a couple of times a week. Of course due to censorship he could not tell me exactly where he was or what was going on but I guessed he was not too far inland and probably in Belgium. Christmas came and went and life continued along in a rather dull sort of way. Things were a little easier for the civilians with the easing of air raids and rockets but rationing and shortages were even worse and just about everybody had somebody in the front line somewhere to worry about. I had lost a young cousin as a midshipman on a lend lease ship that had been sunk in the Atlantic and in the early part of 1945 I lost another young cousin, only nineteen years old. He was the pilot of a fighter-bomber, one of the small fighter panes equipped with just one bomb that were brought into action towards the end of the European war. I think he had only been on one or two missions when he failed to return from one. No trace of his plane was ever found.

In March I got exciting news, Jake was due for leave and hoped to have a whole week in England. I secretly hoped it would be a bit longer as so many of my friends had had their husbands one week extended by several days due to the "traffic jam" across the Channel. Well we were not that lucky it was just one week but we were able to find a place to stay for a few days in Torquay and had a very happy time together. It really looked as though the end of the war was in sight and we were hopeful that in just a few months our separation might be ended. Jake told me that he had turned down the Engineers commission. He felt a bit guilty about it but did not want to face a transfer to the far east with a much longer separation from me than if he stayed in Europe. I could appreciate his guilty feeling but was very glad he had done so.

The next month, in April, came news of Roosevelt's death. I well remember the day as I was walking a little way behind a woman in town when a GI walked towards us. The woman stopped and went up to the GI to commiserate with him on the death of his President. To her amazement he laughed and said "Glad to see the son of a bitch go, bloody Democrat"! So much for politics!

A week after this came the news that Mussolini had been captured by Italian partisans and shot and that the bodies of

Back to London, 1944

he and his mistress were hung upside down in the streets of Milan. Now all was focused on Hitler as Russian troops entered Berlin. On May 1st. it was announced that he was dead and it was believed that he had killed himself. Surrender of all German forces came quickly and on May 8th. the peace treaties were signed, the day henceforth being known as VE Day, Victory in Europe Day.

By chance Hylda and Sylvia came to the house on May 8th, so the three of us dashed up to town to share in the celebration. The streets were crowded with people, everyone hugging everyone else and dancing all over the place.

We had hoped to go to Buckingham Palace to see the King and Queen but the crowds were so intense that it was almost impossible to walk let alone make your way any distance so after an hour or so of soaking up the almost hysterical atmosphere we got to a railway station and made our way home.

I had a letter from Jake a few days later written on VE Day from somewhere in France. He started off by saying that they were celebrating in a big way as one of the planes had just flown in loaded with bottles of champagne that had been "released" from captivity in a German officer's stronghold. As the letter - and the champagne drinking - progressed it seemed everyone in camp had to send me a note and finally it ended with someone writing sideways on the paper "I don't think we can write any more. Jake's asleep". A classic letter.

Of course we still had Japan to reckon with but after Germany's defeat they were pretty weak and in August the atom bomb was dropped bringing immediate surrender. After six years it was finally over.

It was a strange feeling. We sort of expected everything to get back to normal, but what was normal? Certainly the blackout was over, church bells rang again but rationing continued, got worse actually, and the streets were still filled with military uniforms. On a personal level my letters from Jake were still arriving, still censored, but I did know that he was in Germany and trying to get some leave to come to England. That hope faded away and he thought he might be going directly to the States but it was nothing but rumour after rumour. Then there was a longer than usual time between letters and suddenly a letter from America, he was home.

I learned later that it had been a trip not without some problems. They had flown, a convoy of several planes, to Africa first then across to central America and then north. Only one plane made it all the way on schedule. Others broke down at various points along the way and they dribbled in one by one. Jake's plane had a repair layover in Africa and then had a forced landing in central America, a very scary low altitude flight looking for a small emergency airfield that luckily they found.

The plane was unable to continue but another plane was sent to pick the men up and so eventually they arrived in Florida and suddenly Jake was a civilian. He spent a couple of weeks with his family in New Jersey, his mother had died while he was in Europe but later his father had married his former wife's sister-in-law, a widow. Then Jake took the train west planning to find both work in forestry and a place for us to live.

War Brides Travel to America, 1946

Meanwhile the US Government announced plans to give free transportation to the States for "war brides" but it would be quite a while getting organised and when your name came up you would have very little notice. With the war over I was no longer required to work for the Admiralty so I decided to leave there and get a part time job that I could leave at short notice without causing any problems.

I found a part time job as a school secretary, working a few hours a day at the local elementary school. Not really secretarial work, as we know it, mostly collecting and counting milk money (children brought money to pay for the milk they would drink at lunch time) and doing a little general accounting work and running messages for the Principal. I could walk to the school and the work was easy and I did not want to sit around home all day.

Finally in January 1946 I got word that I should go to a briefing in London to find out all about the transportation being provided and I should be on my way in a few weeks. The meeting was not the best, the U.S. Red Cross people ran it and the general impression that I and others got was that they were terribly condescending and that we were on the whole a darn nuisance to them. I knew the GIs in general had very few good words to say for the Red Cross women and after this meeting I must say I agreed with them. I also came away from the meeting wondering if this was going to be the kind of reception I would get from other Americans when I landed. I didn't say much about these thoughts at home as I knew Mum and Dad were not happy about me going anyway.

The last day came. Mum and I tried to make it a peaceful day at home but we were both on edge and the usual routine of touring the shops for perhaps some fish or the elusive Spam had to be continued. The day seemed to drag by hour after hour and then suddenly it was evening and time to pack my two hand cases leaving just my toothbrush to be forgotten in the morning. The guardian angel of toothbrush manufacturers must have been hovering over several English homes that night judging by the number I saw purchased at the camp and on the ship!

And so to bed, the same bed in which I had shivered many a night listening to the doodle-bugs (V-1s) chugging overhead or the staccato explosion of rockets. Well that was over, tomorrow I would start for a land where such things did not exist even as memories. So, finally, I slept.

The next day did not as in novels "dawn bright and clear". The roads were covered in ice and there was a thick fog. The prospect of an army hut on Salisbury Plain was not an enticing one. The taxi we had ordered was late as it had already been on one fog laden trip that morning. It was a cold and miserable journey, we crawled slowly along and in spite of warm clothes and a car rug (blanket) our hands and feet were numb as the car windows were open to allow the driver to see as much as possible in the fog.

I was worried about being late as my orders had told me to report promptly at 9am to the Railway Transport Officer at Waterloo Station. However as any soldier could have told me the army's motto was "Hurry and Wait" and when I made my way through the crowds in the station I was met by blank stares and "Wait outside, we don't know when you are leaving". An hour later I and about four hundred others together with friends and relations were still "waiting outside". The press photographers had been busy and from this time until we arrived in New York we were news with a capital "N".

At last we boarded a special train and it was time to say our final farewells. Many mothers and daughters were in tears but the majority were doing their best to stay cheerful. Mum was wonderful although I will never forget the look on her face as the train finally pulled out. I sat down feeling deflated but in a moment we were besieged by reporters who were travelling to the camp with us and in adjusting to the film star atmosphere for the first time in our lives for most of us we forgot our first pangs.

Halfway through the journey a young corporal came through the train to check our names and he insisted that according to his list I had a young child with me. I pointed out that my husband would be surprised to say the least as I had not seen him for a year but not daunted the corporal grabbed a young child wandering by, planted him next to me and demanded to know if this was "it". Luckily the child's mother came along at that moment to claim the child so the corporal was forced to admit that just possibly his list was wrong. He moved off shaking his head and I settled back having overcome the first hurdle in a trip that was indeed to develop into a kind of obstacle race for those of us unaccustomed to doing things the army method if I dare call their way a "method".

We arrived at Tidworth in the early afternoon, snow was on the ground and dribbled into our shoes as we lined up to wait for a bus to take us to the camp. We were taken into a large hall where we were told to leave our cases and then we were taken into the mess hall. My spirits rose at the thought of a good hot meal. I was cold, hungry and unsure of the future but a good hot meal would help. What I got was a cold miserable excuse for a meal and then we were told to return to where we had left our cases.

After a brief welcome by the camp commandant we were allocated our accommodation. This took most of the afternoon and it was after five by the time I was finally led to my room. We were in brick buildings, four rooms to a building and sixteen beds to each room. Each room had a large coal stove for heating and the German prisoners of war were supposed to keep us supplied with coal. I found that I, at the ripe old age of twenty five, was the oldest in my room, most of the others being under twenty. We were an odd assortment, factory hand, Land Army girl, civil servant, film actress, shop assistants and office workers. There was nothing for us to do specifically that night so we turned in about eight o'clock but I don't think many of us slept much. It snowed all night, the army blankets were thin and the stove went out. Nearby me a seventeen year old cried herself to sleep.

In spite of the cold I must have slept because all too soon it was 6:30 and people were stirring. There was a mad scramble to get washed, we had to collect by fair means or foul an enamel bowl and then take it to the door where some of the prisoners had a vat of boiling water and would dish some out to you. Then it was over to the mess hall for breakfast and we began to think that the Americans were carrying their love of iced things a bit too far when we had two ice cold fried eggs and two pieces of dry ice cold toast.

We had been told to return to our rooms immediately we finished eating as there was a lot to be done so we hurried back and only had a two hour wait until someone turned up to get busy. An officer and NCO came in to inspect our hand luggage. I signed a form declaring that I had no firearms or explosives in my luggage. I was tempted to hint that I had an A-bomb or two but I controlled myself! Of course I would have been unmasked at the next stage of the proceedings as we were marshalled into the reception hall for a medical exam.

The Folies Bergere would have had to look to their laurels if we had cared to go into competition with them but two nurses and one doctor - and a few GIs who just "happened" to wander by were a poor audience. It must have been a comical sight to see a hundred or so girls lined up in their birthday suits with army dressing gowns draped loosely around them and I mean loosely as few of us reached the required measurements to get them to touch where we needed them. Unfortunately we were not much in the mood to see the funny side of the situation.

After this came another long line up to hand in our English money and get dollars in exchange. Lunch then came as a welcome relief from all the endless routine questioning and after that came the final official job of handing in our ration books, both clothing and food. From the number of clothing coupons left in the books I do not think the Boars of Trade got very fat on them. There had been rumours in the papers for some time that we would be getting some extra coupons to outfit ourselves suitably for the cold sea journey but these were just rumours.

That completed the routine for the day and after supper we went to see a movie being shown in the main hall. I forget the title of it, in fact it was completely forgettable. That night we had some extra coal for the fires and warmer and tired most of us slept fairly well.

The two days that followed were boring and exasperating. We had nothing whatever to do and the NCO in charge had asked us not to go into the lounge that the Red Cross had provided in case he needed us for anything. So there we sat, sixteen girls kicking our heels under sixteen beds. The snow had turned to sleet but the fires were pretty good now and we were warm enough, just very bored. We wrote letters home but we did not want people at home to know how miserable we were so the letter writing was not easy. We had a couple of entertainments in the evenings but nothing helped in the daytime.

We had hoped to sail on Friday night but the ship was delayed and we were told that evening that we were to go early on Saturday and we should be up at 5am for breakfast. Poor mutts - we should have known but of course we believed that and lay awake all night afraid we might oversleep.

So Saturday, January 26th., we were all up early and ready to eat so we went over to the mess-hall. No sign of any food and no sign of any Germans, maybe their Union did not allow them to be up before six in the morning. Finally a worried looking sergeant, American not German, appeared and asked what we were doing up so early. He did his best but all we got was a cup of lukewarm coffee. Then we hung

War Brides Travel to America, 1946

about awaiting for something to happen and we were finally loaded on to a train about nine o'clock. In a couple of hours we arrived at Southampton dock and to our amazement there was actually no delay here and we immediately boarded the ship and were directed to our cabins.

After the camp my accommodation seemed wonderful. Of course part of this was due to the fact that the cabins had been allocated alphabetically and as I had been smart enough to marry someone with a "B" name I was on A deck in what had been the first class section of the ship in peace time. In addition to this by sheer luck I had been put in a small "L" shaped cabin so there was only room for two double-decker bunks and one cot. The ship had been newly painted - a fact that we regretted later on - and looked so bright and cheerful that we felt happier than we had since we left home. We had our own shower and wash basin and lavatory and we even had an electric fan so we were in pretty good shape. Many of the larger cabins on this deck held nine women and five babies and on the lower decks things were much more crowded. There were converted hospital wards with 24 to 26 women in them and with very limited toilet facilities.

Two of my cabin mates had been in the same room as myself at Tidworth. One a girl of seventeen who was already very homesick and the other a cheerful girl a year or two younger than myself who was a very good companion to have in these circumstances. The fourth member of our party came into the cabin soon afterwards, a girl about twenty with a ten month old baby.

It was soon time for dinner so we set out to find the dining room. The regular ship's dining room had been reserved for those with babies so we found our way to the improvised troop dining room. The meal was wonderful and after days of cold or lukewarm dull food we all made pigs of ourselves, enjoying not only the good food but the happier atmosphere.

We went on deck after the meal and just before four o'clock the loud speaker began warning all non sailing personnel to go ashore so we went to the port side (we were already getting nautical!) to see the last of the land. It was drizzling with rain, a handful of dockers and officials stood watching, a couple of them waved and we were off. There had been some talk of a civic "Godspeed" for us as we were the first group to leave but when the time came we left without any fanfare. We found later that the big fuss was reserved for the next group as they were going on the Queen Mary.

Supper that night was another superb meal and while we were in the dining room we heard the radio instructions for dropping the pilot and we were really on our way. Then we went to a meeting when we were given a little pep talk by the Transport Commander and then we turned in for our first night at sea. One of my companions was already feeling sick as the boat was rolling quite a bit but I and the other girl patted ourselves on our backs and said we felt fine - oh the pride that goes before the fall.

I awoke very early on Sunday morning. I had no watch but it was still quite dark. I lay for a while feeling the throbbing of the engines going right through me and feeling a bit groggy. I was sure I couldn't be seasick so I couldn't think what it could be.

Soon we were all awake, we got up and dressed, very slowly and carefully and in complete silence. Almost without speaking we made our way to the dining room, the Philippine waiters bustled up with piping hot dishes. Two fried eggs looked at me, I looked back at them and they won. With as much dignity as I could muster and made my way back to the cabin. Our cabin steward advised up to get up on deck and get some air so we went up and wrapped in blankets lay in deck chairs and watched the sea drifting lazily by as at this time it was quite calm.

After a while we had to return to our cabins to prepare for a boat drill that went off very smoothly. I think we were all feeling so rotten we couldn't do anything stupid.

The next day passed in a similar fashion, we went to the dining room but one look at the food or even a sniff of the dining room air and we left with all due haste. The medical staff reported 86% of the passengers were sick and attributed this to the fact that we had all been in such a nervous state to start with, we had eaten very little for the few days before embarking and the first day on board while the ship was in dock we had probably all over eaten. To add to this the ship stank with new paint fumes and very strong disinfectant, both probably very necessary but not helpful to wobbly tummies. Our steward also pointed out that the hold was practically empty (our luggage allowance had been minimal) and that caused the ship to roll more than was normal.

The third day out I began to sit up and take notice. We had a long chat with one of the deck stewards in the morning and he told us that the ship had gone 500 miles off course to avoid a very heavy storm and that we should have a pretty calm voyage now that we had got our sea legs. At least that night I and the others did eat a little dinner, not exactly with relish but without much discomfort. There was a baby show being held in the lounge that afternoon and we went to see it. It was held in the promenade deck lounge and the motion there was much more noticeable so we decided that discretion was the better part and went back to our cabins. Dinner was a few crackers. They were now our staple diet.

In the evening we felt better and risked the lounge again to join in a sing song. One of the wives was a professional singer and led us very efficiently. We followed with plenty of gusto if not much technique. The singing was broadcast so that those who had been unable to come to the lounge could enjoy (?) it in their cabins.

The ship's radio had become an integral part of our lives. Twice a day there was a broadcast of popular music for two hours and each evening there was a broadcast vespers service followed by a sing song. Announcements to both crew and passengers were also given over the air and some of the latter had a humorous touch. One ran "there is a small boy cutting capers outside the purser's office, will his mother please come and rescue the purser". And another "A blue eyed cherub in yellow rompers is in the radio room determined to get on the air, will the mother please collect?" So many babies did in fact get lost that after a day or two adhesive labels were stuck on the nape of each child's neck. We had quite a bit of difficulty in understanding some of the American accents on the radio so after a few days some of the passengers were roped in to act as announcers. We also had a daily newspaper entitled "Wives Whispers" and the most eagerly looked for item each day was the report on how many miles we had covered and how many miles we still had to go.

Tuesday night the storm we had been trying to evade crept up on us and all night long we tossed and shook. I seemed to spend most of the night standing on my head and my cabin mates said they felt the same sensation. The two whose bunks ran in the opposite direction to mine also had to hang on for fear of falling out of their bunks. Early in the morning a warning was broadcast forbidding us to go on deck and advising us to stay out of the corridors because of the risk of being thrown about and injured. Strangely enough now it was really rough I felt much better and for the first time ate large meals and enjoyed them.

During the morning I went down to 'C' deck to see a girl I had become friendly with at Tidworth. She was in one of the converted hospital wards and they were in a pitiable state. Being so crowded the heat seemed so much greater and their room had been flooded in the night so most of their clothing was soaking wet. I believe it was on this deck that one mother awoke to find her baby's cot floating on about six inches of water with the baby chuckling with glee and rocking the "boat". My friend was feeling miserable so I took her up to my cabin where at least she could sit down - her cabin had no chairs - and we could turn on the fan to at least give the illusion of fresh air that we wanted so badly. We could not have the portholes open so the fan did help.

In the evening the storm was even worse. At supper everything kept rolling off the tables but our waiter was equal to it. He poured water over the tablecloths so that most things stuck to the cloth. Even so one lurch dislodged much of the food and more than one person had a bowl of soup or a cup of coffee in her lap while apples and oranges rolled to and fro across the floor.

My cabin mates and I decided to go to the movie that night but we had not bargained for the full programme. First of all there was a not quite up to date newsreel showing action in the Philippines with the commentator pointing out that victory was still a long way ahead. Following this there was a full length film of a football match between the Alabama Somebodies and the New York Somebody-elses. We were no students of American football and this film certainly did nothing to clarify the situation for me. For one thing I had always understood that a ball was used but I did not see one in all the forty five minutes, the men seemed to be very energetically running uphill (maybe the motion of the ship had something to do with this!) and every now and again would stop and put their heads together, presumably trying to decided which way to run next. By the end of the match we were all exhausted and hadn't a clue as to who had won, not that we really cared.

The main film came next something entitled "Out of this World" with Eddie Bracken starring in it. We enjoyed this pretty well partly because of assorted "off stage" developments that helped things along. There was Eddie with I think Bing Crosby's voice crooning to a bunch of swooning bobby soxers and the ship suddenly gave a big roll and a little extra swooning began as a whole row of chairs complete with their occupants slid across the lounge to land in a heap in the corner. The Atlantic certainly showed us it could out-swoon Hollywood.

The next two days passed in a similar fashion, the storm abated a little on Friday and then we ran into snow and fog and so still proceeded very slowly. When we checked the map that showed our progress we found that we had slowed so much that we had only gone 160 miles in the past twenty four hours. On Saturday I awoke feeling that as far as I was

War Brides Travel to America, 1946

concerned they could give America back to the Indians right now and as the day progressed I felt worse and worse. Two of the others in the cabin also succumbed and we were a miserable trio. Actually the ship had passed through the worst weather and was now speeding up to try and get us in New York by Monday and it was the speed that had hit us in our tummies.

We had been advised over the radio to be in our cabins and in our pyjamas for a medical inspection that afternoon. I do not think we shall ever forget it. We had been provided with little "sick" boxes and we were all putting them to good use when in walked the doctor and a nurse. While the doctor examined us the nurse peered over her shoulder and in honeyed tones enquired if we had felt "at all sea sick" on the trip. I wished I had the strength to give her a suitable answer but meekly we all murmured something in the affirmative and restrained from further comment at least until she had left the cabin!

America

The last day dawned and it was a wonderful feeling to think the sea part of the journey was just about over. The evening was exciting, digging out clothes we had not been wearing on board and packing our cases, trying to squeeze in the soap flakes and cigarettes we had bought on board. Our cabin looked like a beauty shop, hair washing, manicuring, face packs and last minute titivating. Finally we shooed any visitors back to their own cabins, finished our packing and tumbled into bed with our minds in a whirl at the thought of meeting our husbands or new relatives tomorrow.

It was bitterly cold that night and none of us slept well. At about three in the morning we heard the orders given over the radio for taking the pilot on board and soon after that came the strains of Deanna Durbin's version of "God Bless America". We tried to peer out of the porthole but it was coated with ice - on the inside I mean! - and too thick to scrape off.

At first we decided it was too cold to go up on deck as we had been urged to do but finally the excitement of the moment got to us and we went up. It was two degrees below zero and pitch dark, the deck was coated with ice and we had to walk very gingerly. As our eyes became accustomed to the dark we could see a few small ships lying at anchor and then we saw a row of brilliant lights and in the distance, growing nearer every minute, the floodlit statue of Liberty. We heard afterwards that the Transport Commander had radioed a request for the statue to be lighted for us as it had been for returning troop ships and we appreciated the gesture. We did not stay up on deck very long as it was so cold, so then we went inside to breakfast - it was 6am.

Three hours later the press was allowed on board and from then on it was every man for himself. The reporters were for the most part very pleasant but we were feeling too tired and jittery to face them so after the first half hour we developed a technique to handle the situation. As soon as a reporter started to come into the cabin we all put a finger to our lips and said "Shh, the baby is asleep" whereupon he or she crept away promising to be back in a little while. Luckily the baby obliged by sleeping for over an hour, the longest sleep of the voyage judging by the noisy nights we had had.

We had lunch at 10:30 and then we assembled in the lounge for a welcoming speech by some of the military personnel. Our passports and visas were inspected for the umpteenth time and then we returned to our cabins to await further orders. I had lost my cabin mates in the crowd and they suddenly came racing to me to say that a list had been up with the names of those husbands who would be waiting for the ship in New York and my husband's name was on the list. We executed an impromptu jig around the cabin for joy. One of the others was so happy to think that she would have company on the trip to Indiana and I was thrilled that Jake was going to be there. It had already been arranged that whether or not he would be there I would spend a few days in his parents' home before proceeding to Washington state but it would be doubly enjoyable with him there. We had not seen each other for almost a year and had in fact only had fifteen days together in our nineteen months of marriage. While we were still chortling with glee some officials came into the cabin to check on our destinations and hang more labels on us until we began to look like Christmas trees filled with decorations. One of my cabin mates had to stay on the ship until late that evening and then they would put her on a train to Michigan and another one had some kind of typical army mix-up as they had her down as going to Florida and she was actually heading to Tennessee. Then came an announcement that those whose surnames began with A or B and who were being met in New York should go immediately to a certain gangway to disembark. I said a hasty farewell and left the cabin, never did find out whether the army won and my friend went to Florida regardless.

We should have known by this time what the army meant by "immediately" as an hour and a half later we were still standing by the gangplank. Eventually about 1:30 the gangplank was lowered and we started off. A tiny army band played "Here comes the Bride", a few flashlights went off and in a few steps we were at last in America.

A bus was waiting to take us to the New York Central Red Cross office where we were to meet our husbands. We piled into the bus and off we went but the driver seemed to be driving at a break neck pace and of course to us was also driving on the wrong side of the street so it was all a bit nerve wracking. Had we survived all the perils of the trip at sea to end up a traffic casualty. But no, we made it in one piece. We followed each other up some stairs and suddenly we were in a room crowded with people and two huge floodlights were shining on us and blinding us completely. I was trying vainly to see Jake in the crowd when a man and woman came up to me and in another minute I was in the arms of my new mother and father. Jake was not there, his

America

father having the same initials the relationship had been confused on the ship's list. I was bitterly disappointed but Mum and Dad did everything they could and as soon as I had been signed for (one baggage received!) and my hand luggage collected we took a taxi to Pennsylvania Station and so home to Hillside, New Jersey, arriving there a little after four o'clock, just twelve hours after the ship had docked that morning.

The first thing I did was to have a lovely long luxurious bath, perfect bliss after two weeks with nothing but cold showers. Then I got into fresh clothes and felt like a new woman. While I was in the bath Mum had cooked dinner and it was ready by the time I came downstairs and it was a delicious meal. Soon after there was a knock on the door and after answering it Mum brought in a huge basket of fruit, covered with cellophane and decorated with pretty ribbons. This was a Welcome to America present from friends of the family. It was such a kind gesture and I enjoyed meeting these people later and thanking them in person.

Later that evening I phoned Jake and it was wonderful to hear his voice though we were both too excited to talk very coherently. He was still 3,000 miles away from me but only land divided us now and in a week or two we would be together. One amusing fact did come out of this conversation. I must have mentioned to someone at some stage of the voyage that Jake had been unable to find any apartment for us to live in and I had joked that we would probably end up living in a wigwam. Whoever I had said this to must have been one of the press travelling largely incognito with us for that rash statement of mine had been published in Seattle and Portland papers as though I had said it very seriously and Jake had been inundated with calls from friends kidding him about it and asking just where he was going to pitch his wigwam.

It was quite late that night when I finally got to bed and I felt it was all too good to be true, a comfortable bed that did not sway all night, as much hot water as I needed and Mum and Dad had got everything for me by my bedside, cigarettes, matches, magazines. I did not need the latter for as soon as my head hit the pillow I was asleep.

The next day we had breakfast early as we had to go to Brooklyn to collect the trunk I had sent before leaving England. I had sent the trunk addressed to my father-in-law, sent him a key and a letter authorising him to open the trunk for inspection but the authorities still would not allow him to collect it without me signing more papers. It had been on the docks about a week then and it had to be collected within a couple of days "or else".

We went by bus into Newark and then took the train to New York. First we had to go to the Custom House and then to the officers of the shipping company and finally got the paper work done. Then we had to find the dock in Brooklyn. We did the grand tour of Brooklyn, we asked a policeman and he had no idea where the dock was, we asked other people and it was like we were travelling through an uncharted region. Well eventually by a stroke of luck we stumbled across the dock we were looking for and were able to finish off the paper work and arrange for the trunk to be delivered to Hillside. That done we headed back to New York City.

I was sort of disappointed in New York. I don't know quite what I had expected but for one thing the skyscrapers did not impress me as I thought they would do. The shops were thrilling in view of the quantities of things that were available and the average New Yorker seemed very well dressed after living with the average Londoner trying to keep clothed with limited supplies and clothes rationing. But even so there was no originality in dress, every woman I saw was wearing black and furs, almost like a uniform. I must admit that I envied the furs, it was bitterly cold and I was feeling it badly. Perhaps this cold and the bleak atmosphere had something to do with my first feelings towards New York. We went into the two most famous churches, the Roman Catholic St. Patrick's cathedral and Trinity Church, both very beautiful in different ways.

The next three days passed in visiting friends and neighbours. The amount of food at dinner parties never ceased to amaze me as did also the lack of knowledge of British rationing. People were astonished when I gave them some of the cold hard facts of rationing. Many of them seemed to be under the impression that we really had no shortage of food the moment the war was over and were rationing as a token of good will towards the rest of hard hit Europe and not because we needed to. As to myself I must confess I enjoyed all the food and I seemed to be always eating. I had lost 7 lbs. since I had left home but I put that back pretty quickly.

We arranged to take a five day trip to see some relations in New York state and also in southern New Jersey but before we started I spent one day on a shopping trip in Newark. I was looking for towels and sheets that were in short supply so we phoned several stores first to find out which stores had them. I also bought myself some gloves, slippers and shoes, the numbers of shoes on sale left me wide eyed with amazement. At the first shop I asked very humbly and dubiously if they had a black court shoe. This was duly translated into "dress" shoe and a selection - yes, a selection! was brought to me. I hesitated between two styles and the assistant went off and came back with a couple more. That was too much for me to take, I hurriedly made up my mind and we went off to lunch. There was one touch of home that day, I had to queue to buy some stockings, but at least I got some.

The three of us left Hillside the next morning and drove to Hamburg in New York state where we stayed overnight with a cousin of Jake's. Their children were in school in Poughkeepsie about 70 miles north of Hamburg so the next day we drove up to see them. It poured with rain all day so from a sightseeing point of view it was not too successful but I did enjoy the sensation of standing on the deck of the ferry crossing the Hudson and watching the ice on the river being broken as the ferry ploughed through.

Our next port of call was to be George School in Pennsylvania, a Quaker boarding school where both Jake and his father had been educated before going into college and where they had friends on the teaching staff. The journey from Hamburg to George School was a very lovely one although the weather did not help. We circled Lake Mohawk and the summer homes looking a little bleak nevertheless made a lovely picture.

When we arrived I was able to look over most of the school and this I did enjoy. I saw all the classrooms and visited some of the dormitories. As at Poughkeepsie the girls shared a room with just one other girl and the rooms looked nicely furnished and comfortable. I met an English girl who had been evacuated in 1939 and was soon to return to England. I reflected how different she would find things on her return.

Before dinner we visited the kitchens, large spotless rooms with huge refrigerators and their own bakery. All the students help in turn to do certain things towards the preparation of the meals. At dinner I noticed even the youngest boys did not seat themselves until all the girls were seated, I suppose today with the Women's Lib culture that has gone by the wayside. After everyone was seated there was a brief silence for Grace and then it was up knives and forks and lets tackle the meal. The chatter seemed about the same as I had heard in our dining hall when I was at school.

I met some of the staff, some of whom had taught Jake seventeen or eighteen years ago and they wanted to know about his experiences overseas. We spent the night in the house of one of Dad's friends and the next day drove to Rancocas, crossing the Delaware at Washington's Crossing en route.

Rancocas is a tiny village in southern New Jersey with a predominately Quaker population and it seemed that in the two days I was there that everyone I met was related to Jake in some way or another. I enjoyed listening to the "plain" language and I was reminded of a story I had heard of two Quaker boys at play. One had been very annoying to the other and after standing it as long as he could the second boy could contain himself no longer. "Oh", he shouted, "Thee little YOU, thee".

The Quaker Meeting House, or I should say the Friends Meeting House was built in 1772 on the site of a former meeting house built in the graveyard in about 1703. The records of all the family histories are kept there and I was asked to fill in the date of our marriage and sign my name in the record book.

Our last stopping place before returning to Hillside was Camden, just over the river on the New Jersey side from Philadelphia. Here I met my new step brother and step sister and I was soon to discover that brothers whether of the English or American variety are much the same as far as teasing goes. That night when the dinner party broke up we drove a guest home, it was about 1am and I was amazed to find that the streets were crowded with traffic and as bright with neon signs as it had been at midday. I had almost forgotten how it felt like to see theatre crowds late on a Saturday night or to see the lights of Piccadilly twinkling at night and I felt like a child with a Christmas tree. I must have sounded like one too with all my "oohs" and "ahs". It was impossible to explain the blackout to people, they just could not comprehend it.

I found myself on several occasions getting rather annoyed with women I met who seemed to think that their "war work" won the war. As far as I could gather their only work was a bit of sewing or fruit bottling while they spent afternoons or evenings at a club. I suppose I should not blame them I am sure they would have done a good job if they had actually been called upon to do so.

On the Sunday we crossed the bridge into Philadelphia as I wanted to see Independence Hall and other famous buildings. I was amused at the reluctance of the family to suggest I go there in case it should seem that they were rubbing in the War of Independence. I assured everyone that what happened 200 hundred years ago did not worry me in the least, most of our colonies were breaking away now anyway so what did it matter if America was the first. I was a little staggered to find when we went into Independence Hall that the attendant and doorman was Australian and had lived in England for several years. I thought Philadelphia was the nicest town I had seen in the east, I suppose partly because it was older and quieter and had an atmosphere that appealed to me much more than the noisy slick New York.

Among other letters awaiting me on our return to Hillside was one that surprised and touched me. I had been interviewed by an Elizabeth newspaper the week before and had touched on the subject of clothes rationing. This letter was from an elderly man who had read the interview and wrote to offer me all the clothes that had belonged to his wife who had died recently. He suggested that I meet him the following Sunday at a certain church, have lunch with his family and collect the clothes. I had to decline the offer as I was leaving for the west coast before that Sunday but it was a sweet offer.

I also had a letter from Jake saying that he had been able to get an apartment. It was only a one room affair but at least I would not have to end up in a wigwam. Although I had enjoyed my stay in Hillside I was very anxious to get going on the last leg of my journey. By a stroke of luck Dad had been able to get reservations through to Portland so I would be leaving Newark on Thursday afternoon connecting with the streamliner in Chicago and arriving in Portland on Sunday morning.

I had three more days in Hillside and on one of these days we went in to New York to go to Radio City. I think this was at the time supposed to be the world's largest amusement place and it certainly was immense. Actually I was not very impressed with either the stage show or the film that was showing but I suppose I just hit a poor week. After the show we went up to the 70th. floor roof to have a look at the city but it was a very misty day and actually we could see very little. We put a nickel in a telescope thing but by the time we had found out how to focus our nickel had run out.

Talking of nickels in slots, something that had amused me a lot on the day of my arrival was that in Pennsylvania Railroad station in New York City there were three prices for admission to the ladies toilets - free, five cents and ten cents. I never did reach the aristocratic status of a ten cent one so I am still wondering if you got a fur covered seat for the extra nickel.

I did a little more shopping, picking up a blouse and some pyjamas for myself but I could not find any men's pyjamas although Jake had asked me to try and get some. I thought perhaps I could shop in the day I had to kill in Chicago. The prices were very similar to those in London and most things for women were in plentiful supply. I suppose the men's clothing supplies had been hard hit by all the returning servicemen looking for civilian clothes. This also affected the supplies of household linens with people now setting up their own homes rather than living perhaps with relatives while their husbands were overseas.

It had begun to snow and by the time we got back to Hillside the snow was about 6 inches thick. We stopped off at some friends for dinner and by the time we left them the snow was now about a foot deep. The bus we should have taken was not running so the friends got out their car and with a lot of pushing and shoving we got it started and they took us home, not very far away actually.

The next day, my last in Hillside was busy. I had my hair done in the morning and then had to tackle the packing. It would be so much easier if one did not have to pack shoes, especially if they have high heels, there is a fortune awaiting a shoe manufacturer who could invent shoes with detachable heels.

We got to Newark station very early but by the time the train actually left it was almost four o'clock. They served dinner fairly early and it was a very ordinary not too attractive meal. The train was acceptable but rather grubby looking although the bed linen was clean.

I did not sleep too well and awoke very early. After partly dressing in my berth I sallied forth in my robe to go to the dressing room to finish my toilet. Here a catastrophe befell me, the door of the toilet jammed and I was neatly trapped inside while the train rushed on. I was annoyed at first, then I saw the funny side of it and began to giggle envisioning the headline somewhere "G.I. Bride Locked in Loo", then I finally began to get a bit worried as I simply could not get out and who would know where I was? Finally after quite a long time someone came into the dressing room and heard me banging on the door so she rang for a porter. He had quite a job getting the door open but I was finally free - and embarrassed!

I decided not to have breakfast on the train as it was still very early and I would have all day to kill in Chicago. I knew I had to go from one station to another but had no idea how to do this. As soon as I stepped off the train I was besieged with porters and before I knew quite how it happened my suitcase was being dashed along the platform in one direction and I was being forced along the other way by the crowd. I managed to break away and asked another porter for help. He looked at me as though I was talking a foreign language (I was!) and did not answer me. Then I asked a man at a booking office what I had to do and he said I had to get some kind of a transfer but then waved me on. Finally I caught sight of my luggage on a trolley and there was a Red Cross girl standing nearby so I asked her if she could tell me where to get the transfer. She snapped, "No", picked up her bags and walked away.

I asked the porter who had my luggage where I should go and he led me to a taxi that apparently was the "transfer". There were about six of us in the taxi, among them the Red Cross girl I had just appealed to for help. She was busy telling a friend how many times she did this trip and how well she knew all the ins and outs. Well perhaps she too had not understood me.

Arriving at the other station I checked my luggage and then decided it was breakfast time. I was utterly confused by all the station clocks not knowing a thing about eastern versus central time but my stomach told me it was breakfast time. After breakfast I went outside the station and managed to follow a policeman's "two blocks north and then one east" without mishap. Americans are the most directional minded people I know and after all I was used to saying "about a tuppenny bus ride on a number 67" if asked for directions.

I found Marshall Field's the largest shop in Chicago but was rather disappointed as according to all the glowing reports I had heard I expected something more magnificent. I think the average American seemed to think we Brits were still in the stone age as someone in New Jersey had been very careful to tell me that in their stores they had escalators and was utterly amazed when I said well of course we did too. They were also amazed, and somewhat disbelieving when, in answer to some question, I had said that London had regular TV broadcasts before the war, long before they had them in the U.S.

It was bitterly cold in Chicago and snowing lightly so just to get out of the cold and to kill time I went into a cinema, it was a strange feeling sitting in there just as if I was at home and I had to remind myself that I was actually in Chicago, gangster Heaven.

Back at the station I had another meal and cleaned up a bit and before long I was boarding the train. As soon as the porter made up the berths I got inside and read and wrote some letters before falling off to sleep. This train in contrast to the other was spotlessly clean, everything sparkling.

I was as hungry as a hunter when I awoke in the morning and the girl in the next berth asked me if I would have breakfast with her. The dining car was at the other end of the train and to get there we had to walk through fourteen compartments, a good way to work up an appetite. Here again the difference between this train and the other was marked. On each table was a vase of flowers and at the end of the dining car was a comfortable alcove where you could wait if all the tables were full. As we ate breakfast we were passing through Nebraska and by the time we had finished we ran into Cheyenne in Wyoming.

I got out to stretch my legs for a few minutes in Cheyenne and then we were on our way again. Soon after the train started a porter came through the train calling my name and to my delight I had a cable from Jake. It was a wonderful feeling to know that even here sort of in the middle of nowhere we could keep in touch. The cable warned me not to jump off at any nearby wigwam - how that remark would haunt me!

The day was pretty boring, the country dull and uninteresting, I was very glad that Jake did not hail from Wyoming. I had beef for dinner that night, enough meat to feed a family of four for a week on England's rations. I went into the lounge after dinner and to celebrate the fact that tomorrow Jake and I would be together I ordered a drink. The steward was very sorry but Wyoming was a "dry" state so I could not have a drink. The girl next to me asked why were other people drinking and we were told that although we could not be sold a drink the steward could "give" us one and we could reimburse him tomorrow when we would be in Idaho. Ah the ingenuity of the bootlegger. So we had our drinks.

Newlyweds Reunite, Longview, Washington

That night I slept well and as I ate my breakfast we passed Bonneville Dam and soon an air of expectation and bustle began to sweep through the train. At 10.45am, exactly on time we ran into Portland. I got out and turned to follow the crowd out to where people were waiting held in check by railway officials, then a figure darted out from behind the restraining hands and in a moment I was clutched in Jake's arms, my hat was on the back of my head, everyone was grinning and I didn't give a darn - it was wonderful.

We had just missed the hourly bus to Longview so we decided to have a cup of coffee. Neither of us drank much, we didn't even talk much just looked at each other and grinned. We caught the next bus and were on our way quickly in pouring rain. The apartment was close to the bus stop so in a few minutes after the bus dropped us off I was finally home.

Home was a tiny one room apartment with a kitchen alcove and bathroom. The bed swung out from a cupboard and came down into the living room at night, that intrigued me immensely, at first I had visions of it swinging back into place with us still in it but all the time we used it nothing disastrous happened so I guess it had been well trained. Anyway we were lucky to have any kind of living place at all.

Jake had the next day off so we went out to do some shopping and acquaint me with Longview. It was still pouring and very gloomy looking but just before we went out a delivery arrived for me, a bouquet of flowers from one of Jake's friends welcoming me to Longview, what a very nice gesture that was. While we were out we encountered a local news reporter who recognised Jake and asked us if he could come and get some photos and a report later that afternoon. You can imagine how tickled we were the next day to find ourselves on the front page of the paper with such minor items as strikes and peace conferences tucked away on the back page. I was the first English wife to arrive in Longview although an Australian wife had arrived sometime before.

The next few weeks passed by quickly. Longview was a very small town so I had no difficulty in finding my way around and no problem choosing where to shop - not much choice. I found the money no problem although at times I was surprised at relative values. Mostly of course I was enjoying myself revelling in all the things available - one notation in my diary of that time simply read, "Bought two dozen eggs!!!!!!!!"

Many Americans complained to me about shortages but to me there did not seem to be any worth mentioning. Sugar was rationed (slightly) and butter was hard to get but that was all. For some reason, no-one seemed to know why, the sale of margarine was prohibited in Washington State but so many people regularly drove into Portland once a week to do their shopping to avoid paying the Washington 3% sales tax and they would pick up margarine there.

All this time Jake and I were hunting for a car, not purely as a luxury but because Jake was job hunting for a better job and for that a car was a necessity. We spent hours and a small fortune in taxi fares tearing around after advertised cars but

Newlyweds Reunite, Longview, Washington

all we saw were wrecks and certainly not worth the prices being asked. This was the first time I had come up against the regulations of the OPA. This government law was supposed to regulate prices on many things including used cars, but it was obviously a farce as all the prices we saw were far above OPA limits so we would not pay them. We finally decided to go to a licensed dealer as the prices there were fixed but in hindsight we would have been better off to pay the inflated price and get a better car, we paid more for repairs etc. than the extra cost would have been. How Jake missed his 1941 Packard he had sold when he was called up!

During my first weeks I had a few adventures shopping, generally due to the shopkeeper not understanding me. One of the funniest incidents was when I set out to buy a pudding basin. Before we were married Jake had unexpectedly come to the flat that I shared with my three friends in Bath. That day we had decided that we wanted something nice to eat so we had pooled our rations of sugar etc. and I had made a sponge pudding. Jake loved it, said it was that that made up his mind as far as marrying me, so I was anxious to cook him another one but for that I needed a pudding basin. At the first shop the assistant looked very vague, muttered something and shook her head. At the second shop I was greeted with a puzzled stare and "No, we don't keep them". The third person was very helpful, she did not have them but if I went to the shop at the end of the road she was sure they could help me. So I went there only to find that it was a plumbing appliance shop and the only basins they had were strictly for bathroom use! When Jake came home I told him of my tough day expecting some words of comfort. What did I get? "Well" said my loving spouse" exactly what is a pudding basin?" Incidentally it took me years to get a basin, and then I got it in Canada.

Of course I should add that Jake had his disappointments too, I would tell him he was having a certain thing to eat that day and it would turn out to be something quite different, we just didn't speak the same food language.

Jake was very anxious to visit some friends in Seattle whom he had not seen since his return from Europe and he also wanted to look over the job market. Currently he was working in the lumber mill in Longview, shift work that was inconvenient to say the least, particularly as when he had to work the night shift he needed to sleep in the day and the bed put down for his sleeping meant that I had about a two foot space in which to spend the day. So at the beginning of March we set out for Seattle.

We had to set out after dark as Jake had worked the day shift and so we could not see too much as we travelled north. It was about a three to four hour drive and to me after so many blackout years driving in the dark was wonderful as every small town we went through was lit up with neon signs. We got into Seattle a little after midnight and that was enchanting too with lights everywhere, so different from little Longview with its one traffic light. We found a hotel room and no sooner were we asleep than I heard a siren and woke up Jake saying "we had better get down to the shelter". He pointed out that we were not in London, the war was over and I had better get used to fire engines!

We spent two days in Seattle and we both enjoyed being in a larger city again. I liked Longview but I did miss the bustle of a bigger place. I had hoped to perhaps see some theatre performances but they seemed sadly lacking, nothing

Newlyweds Reunite, Longview, Washington

much available except the usual movies. We did go out one evening to go dancing but just having picked the place from the telephone directory it wasn't what we wanted. We did enjoy dancing together again but the place was pretty tacky and the music poor, food not bad though.

Jake suggested that we return to Longview by the coastal route so early on Tuesday morning we took the ferry to Port Ludlow and set out in the early misty morning. I really had a far greater sense of adventure than when I set sail from England. I had not yet seen the mountains as it had been foggy or cloudy all the time we had been in Seattle although I knew from everybody I talked to that "just behind the clouds are the mountains".

We drove through the Olympic Peninsula, even the torrential rain could not entirely mar the beauty of the landscape, occasionally the mountains coming into view through the clouds and we passed blue lakes and dense green forests.

Late in the afternoon we arrived in Beaver, the little logging town that Jake had been in before the war and Jake decided that we should go straight to the camp and spend the night there. One of Jake's friends came down from the camp on a speeder to pick us up. The speeder is a petrol driven van that runs on rails rather like a railway line. It has an opening on either side as a doorway and inside a narrow form runs along for seating. Chet had had the forethought to bring a rug down for me, partly to make the seating more comfortable and partly for warmth as it was pretty cold and the trip to camp was seven miles. On the way down Chet had seen some bear and a cougar and I hoped they would be around on our return trip. The driver of the speeder was an Indian named

Oscar Washington and he being the first Indian I had encountered I was sort of disappointed. Where was the lithe and strong Indian of the Hopalong Cassidy stories, this one was short, fat and flabby.

Chet said we were nearing the place where he had seen the bear so he asked Oscar to slow down a bit as we went over a small bridge by a garbage dump. The speeder came almost to a standstill and I went to the open doorway and looked out. There immediately below us was a mother bear and two cubs, the cubs the loveliest little things, black furry bundles with beady little eyes and shiny black noses. I could have watched them for ages but Mummy bear got wind of us and turned towards us and with one accord the three men jumped to the starter and we hastily rattled away. Jake told me that a mother bear, normally fairly placid, will immediately attack if she feels she has to defend her cubs and although she looked rather slow and cumbersome she would only take a couple of minutes to reach the speeder and take care of all of us. Jake also told me many interesting yarns about the bears raiding the logging camps. They love pork and are always raiding the camps storage area, many times bending the steel netting to get at the meat. I had hoped to also see the cougar but we did not see it, they are very seldom seen anywhere near any habitation.

When we got into the camp we went into the cookhouse for a meal, most of the loggers had already eaten but the cook rustled up a meal for we four and the cook hearing that I was English made tea just for me, about two quarts of it! I don't even like tea but for the honour of England I did my best to get some of it down, I appreciated the cook's kind thought.

Newlyweds Reunite, Longview, Washington

Jake and I slept in a little room off the camp office, it was nice and warm as the stoves were kept going all night - no shortage of wood for the fires. Lights out was at nine o'clock and at 5.30 in the morning a whistle blew and that meant the day had started for everyone. We splashed our faces with cold water and went in to breakfast. I was the only woman there with about seventy men including many Indians but no-one showed any curiosity. There was a huge meal piled up, eggs, steaks, toast etc. and everyone set to in silence and as the tables emptied the men went off to work.

The speeder had to go down to the road to pick up mail at 6.30 so we went on it, collected our car at Beaver and set out on our return trip to Longview.

We made a brief detour to visit the Indian village of LaPush in the Quillayute reservation, it was still very early in the morning and there was practically no-one to be seen. We wandered down to the water's edge - my first glimpse of the Pacific ocean - and inspected some of the boats but LaPush too had moved with the times and the canoes had outboard motors. There is an interesting theory about these Indians, it is said that they are closely allied to the Japanese through inter marriage with the Japanese fisherman who used to come to fish off the coasts here. How true this is I do not know but they certainly do have a slightly oriental look, their skin a little more yellow than tanned.

The drive down the coast from LaPush was very lovely and we stopped several times to relax and enjoy the views. We stopped at Ruby Beach where one is supposed to be able to find rubies amongst the pebbles - needless to say we did not find any. We also stopped at Destruction Island, so named after a Spanish adventurer had his boat destroyed and his men massacred by the Indians in 1775 at this point.

We got back to Longview early in the evening, it had been a very enjoyable trip although we had not had any luck in the job market, everything in the logging industry was slow and all the jobs filled with ex-servicemen.

A week after our return we visited a former boss of Jake's who was at that time living about 100 miles north of Longview. It was a pleasant drive and I had my first sight of Mt. Rainier, certainly a magnificent and inspiring peak. By the end of the day Jake had agreed to take a job for Roy that was centred in the Tillamook Burn in Oregon. Not exactly close to Longview but he thought he had better give it a try.

For the next six weeks our life together was just a series of weekends with long gaps in between. Jake would try and leave for home as soon as he got through work but it would be close to midnight by the time he arrived in Longview on a Friday evening and he had to leave early Sunday afternoon to get there for work on Monday morning. We were both doing some serious thinking about what the future held if Jake stayed with logging. His degree was in forestry but jobs for foresters were few and far between and logging jobs although available were by necessity in far off areas with generally speaking poor living conditions. In almost every case the choice would be living in a small town a long way from the logging camp and the logger would only get home at weekends or having the wife move closer to camp probably in a very small house with few if any other women nearby.

Neither of these alternatives appealed to us. Jake had even before the war been thinking of entering some other field and so we began to sit down together and really think

Newlyweds Reunite, Longview, Washington

things out. In various logging camps Jake had done the bookkeeping and he felt that accounting was a profession that had unlimited opportunities. He had enough experience to get a basic job and then would go to evening school to study with the eventual goal of becoming a C.P.A.

The next major decision was whether we should stay in Longview or whether we should move to a larger city with probably better job prospects. Jake was in favour of Seattle and from what little I had seen of it I thought it would be a pleasant place to live. So we took the bull by the horns, gathered everything we had together and set out for the big city. Actually we did leave things behind with friends to be picked up later when we had found somewhere to live in Seattle but mentally we were through with Longview.

Seattle

Our first week in Seattle went by with nothing but depressing results, Jake had a couple of job interviews but nothing definite and apartments were non existent. Towards the end of the week we went over to Bainbridge Island to look at some war housing that might be available, better than nothing possibly although not exactly convenient if Jake did get a job in Seattle as it was a 45 minute ferry ride. We got back to the mainland hotel feeling pretty glum, picked up our mail and there between the letters was a slip with a message asking Jake to call one of the people with whom he had had an interview the early part of the week. It was early afternoon by then but Jake called them right away, they talked briefly and the deal was made, Jake was to start work with the company on Monday.

That evening we decided to treat ourselves a bit instead of looking for housing. Most hotels at that time had a maximum of seven nights stay as so many people were house hunting and living in hotels. So we went to an early show and then went for a drive around the city. Even though we were out for amusement needlessly to say we kept our eyes open for any rental signs and just before turning back to the hotel we saw IT!

The place was pretty miserable but better than nothing so we paid a months rent and moved in the next morning so that Jake could start to work. Three days later we had a stroke of luck and found a better place. We had a very hard time convincing the owner that we would be good tenants,

Seattle

promised not to throw wild parties (who did we know in Seattle), wouldn't dream of having children and had in fact no desire in life short of paying her rent on time and being as quiet as mice any time we happened to be in the apartment. It was not exactly a Heavenly place, our room looked out on a brick wall and we were sandwiched between a bus garage, with busses running all night and a laundry with machinery carrying wood-chips to the furnace on a conveyor belt that also ran most of the night. Later we began to hate the dump but at that time we were thrilled to have somewhere to call our own - sort of our own - and Jake was busy with his new job and beginning to study.

The next weekend we drove down to Longview and bamboozled a friend into helping us move all the rest of our belongings to Seattle.

The next day was a busy one, putting things into the apartment, setting aside some other things that we would have to put into storage and Jake getting ready to start work. The day was just a forerunner of the next couple of weeks, getting organised during the day but having time in the evening to go out, visit friends of Jake's from his pre-war logging industry days or go to a show. And we still spent much time looking for a better apartment.

Eventually the apartment hunting paid off and after a few weeks we moved into a nicer apartment and were able to get our things out of storage. Jake was settling into his job and checking into the accounting courses that he wanted to take. I decided that I would look for a job also, we needed the cash and I was bored sitting in the small apartment all day with very little to do.

A War Bride's Memoirs

I followed up on ads in the paper and went for a couple of interviews. One day I had an appointment with a dentist for a part time receptionist position and as I was early I decided to go across the street to a department store and have a cup of coffee at their snack bar. While I was seated the waitress removed someone's milk shake from the mixer before the beaters had stopped and I got splashed all over with chocolate milk shake. So much for dressing to impress a potential employer. We tried to wipe it all off and they promised to pay any dry cleaning bills I might have but I still felt a bit messy looking. Anyway it could not have been too bad as I did get the job, five days a week, eleven to four.

The week after I started to work was Labour Day weekend and we decided to drive over to Idaho to visit some friends of Jake's whom he had not seen since before the war. We had a very nice weekend and to add to the fun on the way home we stopped at Ellensburg to see their big annual rodeo. First one I had ever seen (don't get too much cowboy activity in London!) and I really enjoyed it.

We settled down into a routine of Jake's work and study and my work and weekends we started to look for some property as Jake was very anxious for us to build our own home. We didn't waste much time, before long we found what we wanted a little way out of town and before the end of the month we were the proud - and nervous - owners of three acres of wooded land for which we paid $1,500.

So now Jake began to draw house plans. He was thinking of a log house, not a primitive log cabin, a regular house but using the logs for the exterior. We went out to the land one day and he felled a tree and peeled it to show me how we could prepare the logs though of course they would have to

Seattle

age before being used in construction. This sort of set the pace for our weekends now, if it wasn't raining we would go out to the land and start clearing it. Jake would fell trees and I got to be pretty expert at peeling, using a draw knife and a peavey to move the logs. The trees averaged forty to forty-five feet high.

During the next year we moved a couple of times, once to a nicer apartment, nicer but pretty small and then to a ramshackle house on the shore of Lake Washington as it had two bedrooms and more space that we needed as Mum was coming for a visit.

Mum's visit was great, we took many trips, each weekend going somewhere that was as often new to me as it was to Mum. We went to the rain forest on the peninsula and of course to Mt. Rainier and Mt. St. Helens and took a little longer trip down the Oregon coast. I remember one day as we were out we were discussing shake roofs, Mum had never heard of them, and passing a rather run down neighbourhood Jake pointed to one house and said "See Mum, that's a shake". She looked at it carefully, smiled sweetly and said, "Oh, I see what you mean but in England we call them "shacks"!

I was looking for a full time job, not too happy with the dentist I was working for, and I got one by a strange chance. Mum and I were talking with the mailman, a very pleasant person, and he said that his wife was nursing director at one of the main Seattle hospitals and she was looking for someone to work in the Nursing Office and do the necessary clerical work. I applied for the job when Mum went home and was able to start in right away.

The firm that Jake was working with were involved with real estate and we began to look for a house. We still planned to build our own but we knew it would be a long time before that could be accomplished. We had incidentally given up on the idea of a log house, we found getting a mortgage for that type of construction would be impossible. We had felled and peeled 70 - 80 trees and eventually we sold them to someone who did plan to build a log cabin on some land they owned on one of the islands.

So in 1948 we bought a house in the north end of Seattle, a small two bedroom house in a pleasant residential neighbourhood. Paid $12,000 for it, average price, not cheap, in 1948. Of course Jake's salary was under $400 a month and I made less than half that.

There had been a couple of small earthquakes and in one a school had been damaged and the company doing the repair work had advertised used bricks for sale. We bought a truckload and Jake went to work building a small brick wall across the front of the house, really improving its appearance. My share of that job was to clean all the used bricks, scraping off mortar and using muriatic acid when necessary. I didn't realise then that I was just getting in practice for a much bigger used brick job on our new house.

In the summer of 1949 our friends, Roman and Edith Mostar asked us to join them in a car trip to Banff and Lake Louise. It was a great trip except for the first time in my life I was car sick from time to time. Couldn't figure it out until I realised it wasn't the car motion it was the fact that I was pregnant! It did not spoil the trip, made it quite exciting and there along in February 1950 came Roger and I became a full time Mum and housewife.

Seattle

Mum came over again, had to see the new grandchild of course and my brother, Doug, came too for a portion of the time. Jake had finished off a room in the basement so we had another bedroom and that made it easier. Jake and Doug went off for a week hiking and they walked completely around Mt. Rainier, had a great time. Mum and Doug went home on the Queen Mary, did not realise then how historic that would become.

Jake's Dad also stopped by briefly on his way to a Boy Scout conference in California. He too was excited to see the first grandson.

Jake was still studying and taking the correspondence courses and taking the CPA exams bit by bit. Every day after work he would go down to the basement and study for two or three hours. Three years after Roger's arrival another son, who we named Doug, arrived on the scene so I was kept fairly busy and of course on weekends we still went out and continued some of the land clearance etc. as we knew we would still build out there when the time was right.

In 1954 we decided that we should sell the house and move into an apartment as we needed the cash to be able to have a down payment and get a mortgage to build the new house. We sold the house without too much trouble, moved into a small apartment, got a mortgage deal signed and then really went to work on the construction. Most weekends we were out there, I would drive Jake out and do a few odds and ends like brick cleaning! - and then bring the boys home for lunch and a nap and then go out again later in the afternoon. And from time to time friends of Jake's would go out and help too. Of course we had professional help too for things such as the pouring of cement for the basement but we enjoyed doing what we could.

In January 1955 we came home on a Saturday, picked up our mail and barely glanced at it as we wanted to get the boys fed and to bed. Then we took time to look at it and there was the super news that Jake had passed the last section of the CPA exam, he was now a CPA. Talk about excitement! It also meant that the hours he had spent studying could now be spent on the house and he started working on the water system. In fact when the city approved his plumbing (all done with the aid of a 25 cent handbook from Sears!) he said he was as proud of that as of his CPA.

In May I picked up Jake on a Saturday and we decided to stop at a drive-in for hamburgers on the way home. I had just got over a cold and both the boys had had sniffles so we felt we could be lazy over the meal and hit the sack early that evening. The next day the boys and I were fine but when Jake came home from work he said he had felt awful all day and was going to bed. I talked him into going out to vote first as there was a special measure on kindergartens that would be helpful to us but as soon as he came home from that he went to bed, most unusual for him.

I had dinner with the boys and got them to bed, checked in on Jake but he was sleeping. Then late in the evening he called me into the bedroom and said get me to the hospital I am going to die. He looked awful but not as if he had a fever or anything but it was so unlike him to not be well that I did call the doctor. He said there was a lot of flu going around, I should take him to the hospital and he would call them with instructions. I called my neighbour, Dorothea and asked if their oldest daughter, Carol, could come over and baby sit while I took Jake in. I went to the hospital where I had worked and they said the doctor had called in and they suggested that I come in about ten the next morning when he should be ready to go home.

The next morning I called Carol to sit again but when I got to the hospital I spoke to my former boss, the Director of Nursing, and she said they had not been able to rouse Jake so I had better wait until the doctor came in and some test results had come.

I called Carol and asked her to stay longer and about an hour later Dorothea arrived, said she thought I might need some company. I surely did for the doctor had just told me that Jake was in a coma and his condition was critical. They wheeled a huge oxygen thing into his room in case it should be necessary and there was nothing for me to do but wait and see what happened as the day went on.

Dorothea said she thought we should go out and get a bite to eat for lunch, we did not want to eat at the hospital cafeteria and there was a small eating place just a block away. It turned out to be rather a funny incident, in retrospect of course. Just before we left the hospital another doctor had come by and said they were pretty sure that Jake had encephalomyelitis and the coma could go on for days, maybe for the rest of his life. So Dorothea and I started to eat and then we looked at each other and we both began to cry. The waitress bustled over and said "Is something wrong with the food?" We assured her that the food was not making us cry but we thought we had better leave. She practically hustled us out, crying eaters not good for business, but she would not let us pay for the food!

The next few days were all the same, I would get a sitter for the boys, go to the hospital and sit around all day, talking to a doctor now and again and waiting for something to happen. After a week Mrs Moody talked to me and said I should see about getting Jake transferred to a VA hospital as this situation could go on for weeks. The hospital bills were already tremendous and they could go on for ever. Both the boys and I had been tested and we did not have the bug, it was probably due to a disease carrying mosquito and we had not been bitten. The doctor said that Jake could have picked it up in Africa where it was very prevalent. He had been in Africa on his way home from Germany at the end of the war. Apparently the bug could lie dormant for years and then be triggered by just a mild cold infection.

Later on when Jake was in the VA hospital and at Mrs Moody's suggestion I did bring the Africa possibility up to one of the doctors there but they scoffed at the idea. Too bad, I might have got a service related pension. I had to start looking for work, Jake had one months pay for sick leave and we would have no income. Luckily Mrs Moody said she would be happy to have me back working for her as her present girl had just quit. It was a very lowly paid job but it was something to start with and I would have to get someone to look after the boys of course.

As it turned out Jake was in a coma for six weeks and in the VA hospital for a year. Mum came out for a couple of months to help me and when she went home I found a nursery school for the boys. The bank with whom we had the mortgage was getting pretty nasty insisting that they talk to Jake and not taking my word for it when I said he was in a coma. Through some of the people Jake had worked with I got in touch with a contractor and he said he could finish the house for the money available and he went to the bank and got their OK to do it.

I was looking for a better paying job, there was no Social Security for disability back in those days and I really had to make more money. After a while I found a job with the Seattle School District in the accounting department, going out to schools to audit their internal books and paying contractors working on various schools.

I tried to visit Jake a couple of times a week, the VA hospital was a long drive, the other side of town and I couldn't afford baby sitters very often. I took the boys out a couple of times but it was very hard on them, Jake was in a wheelchair but strapped in so that he would not fallout, and his speech was so bad that it was very hard to understand anything he said. The nursery school teacher told me she always knew when Roger had visited his Dad because he was always belligerent in class trying to pick fights the day after he had made the visit, so it was obviously upsetting him.

In November Jake started coming home for weekends, I would pick him up Friday evening and take him back to the hospital on Sunday night. He was of course anxious to see how the house was progressing so we would drive out to see it, perhaps clean a few bricks and let the boys pick up various things so that they were participating.

Lake Forest Park, 1956

So eventually in May of 1956 we moved in, our dream house not exactly the dream we had envisioned and a dream that turned into a nightmare when it was found that the contractor had not paid many bills and we began to have liens put against the house. Happily two of Jake's old college chums came to our rescue with loans so we could get the things straightened out and set up a repayment schedule. We did eventually sue the contractor but lost the suit, the bank refusing to speak on our behalf as they did not like to get involved with "this type of messy business".

Roger was now old enough to leave nursery school and to start going to Lake Forest Park elementary school. I found a caretaker near the school and would drop him off there on my way to work. He could walk from her house to school when they opened in the morning and back to her after class, staying with her until I picked him up on way home from work. Doug was still in the nursery school where I would drop him off in the morning. Roger was so unhappy with the arrangement, so many mornings he was crying when I dropped him off and I felt so badly but it had to be done.

Eventually Jake, in his wheelchair, was released from the hospital and with him at home we no longer had to have part time pre school care for the boys.

A man Jake had worked for pre war when he was working in forestry heard of our dilemma and offered to loan us some money if we needed it and actually sent us a cheque as a loan. We thanked him but returned the cheque as we did

Lake Forest Park, 1956

not need it as we had already borrowed from two of Jake's college pals and had been able to repay those loans over the past couple of years.

To our amazement the cheque came back and we were told that it was not a loan but a gift and that I was to use it to take a vacation, go visit my parents as they thought I badly needed a break. I certainly could use one but I couldn't quite see leaving the boys and Jake alone but to my amazement friends and neighbours all insisted I should do it and said they would keep an eye on things and make sure Jake had any help he needed.

So I decided to take the trip, I filled the freezer with every kind of food I could make and left written menus for each day with also written instructions as to how to cook each meal. I also got little gifts for each boy - all three of them! - and hid them around the house so that each week they could look for something.

This was my first visit home since my arrival in the USA in 1946 and it was a wonderful trip. To my amazement Mum and Dad had also decided I really needed a break and they had booked a tour for the three of us to take a bus trip in Europe; France, Switzerland and Belgium. It was a very happy time and the best thing of all was meeting so many friends that I had not seen for fifteen years. And letters came from Jake telling me which friend had had them in for dinner and how things were going so I knew all was well with them.

When I got home my first priority was to find a better paying job and I heard of a vacancy in Allstate Insurance Company. The job was in the Seattle regional office so I applied for it, passed the exam and got the job and started there in March 1961. Rather a dull job to start with but opportunities there for advancement and advance I did in the next twenty plus years!

Another excitement came in 1962. The World's Fair was held in Seattle and Mum and Dad decided to come out and visit us, the first visit to the U.S. for Dad. We drove to the airport to pick them up and as we were getting in the car in the parking lot an announcement came over the loudspeaker that Mrs Avis should return to the Customs section. Mum was so tired that Dad said he and I would take care of it, Mum should stay in the car with Jake. We went to the Customs and found that Mum had left her purse there. We could not take it but one of the Customs men said he would take it to the car to save Mum the walk in. When we got to the car the official asked Mum to check inside her purse to make sure that everything was there but she did not want to do it. Dad and I could not figure her out and the official was getting a bit anxious but finally she did open the purse quickly, looked inside and said everything was OK. When the official left Mum started to cry and then explained what the problem was. She had taken several of the little packages of sugar that come with a meal as she thought the boys would enjoy them but with the Customs man there she thought she would be in big trouble for stealing them! We explained that the little packages whether sugar, salt or pepper were part of the meal and had been paid for whether we used them or not, so it was perfectly acceptable to take them if she wanted to - Welcome to America!

We had a very happy visit. I took some vacation time off and we took several trips to Mt. Rainier and Mt. St. Helens and to the Olympic Peninsula. And of course a visit to the World's Fair. Not the best weather unfortunately but who

Lake Forest Park, 1956

expects that on vacation. Jake did not come with us to the Fair as back then there was no handicapped parking and it was hopeless to try and get in. Mum and Dad enjoyed the trip and Dad was especially happy to see his grandsons for the first time.

The next big family decision was to decide whether the boys should go to George School, the Quaker high school in Pennsylvania. Both Jake and his Dad had graduated from there and they wanted the boys to go. We contacted the school and applied for a scholarship for Roger. He had to take an examination but he passed with no problems and a scholarship was awarded that would cover the cost of tuition, board and room but of course we still had to come up with the expense of transportation, a rail trip from Seattle to Philadelphia. My job at Allstate was at that time on a lower level so I got paid for overtime and I made sure I could work as much extra time as possible to help out the budget.

Starting to check things out, train fares etc. we came up with a better idea and that was to have Jake and the boys drive there, Jake wanted to see his father and with both boys to help it should not be too bad. They could camp out some nights and others find a local inn. The boys were pretty excited about this idea and they set off with me waving "goodbye" with my fingers crossed. This was September 1964.

Actually the trip went very well and it was a great experience for the boys, especially Roger. They stayed with Jake's folks for a few days then they all drove to George School, got Roger settled in and then left him there and Doug and Dad drove back to Seattle, arriving home tired but happy.

Now of course we could not wait for the first letter from Roger and we settled into a routine of getting letters bringing us up to date on the things going on at George School, how the soccer team was going and how Roger's finances were going. He seemed to be happy in the new environment and made friends easily.

The first year he went to the grandparents in New Jersey for Thanksgiving but we were able to have him come home for Christmas and that was excitement for all of us. Roger's first long train ride, quite exciting with a train change in Chicago.

And so life settled down in a routine for all of us, Roger in George School, Doug in the local school and me working. My job was going along well, a couple of promotions that brought a few privileges of rank and more pay. That certainly helped.

When Doug got to the right age, he also qualified for a scholarship and the two of them set off by train together. Although we never heard any complaints from Roger I think at times he really felt the lack of money when so many of his companions had plenty of cash, several of them having their own cars at school for example. He was doing well in sports, winning awards for cross country and actually running in the Boston Marathon with the school's coach. Also doing well in scholastic courses but I just had a feeling all was not right. Just a mothers hunch.

But life was going too easily for us and out of the blue, no previous complaints, no hints of any kind we were notified that Roger had been expelled for disobeying some rules set up for dormitory curfews. He and some other students had been outside the dorm after curfew with some

Lake Forest Park, 1956

female students. Jake's Dad went to the school to pick up Roger and he was furious with the school - the school he adored - saying they were making a mountain out of a molehill, a new principal tossing his weight around.

Roger came home as soon as we could get the trip organised on the earliest train. We enrolled him in the nearest school - Shorecrest High School - for the short time before graduation. Doug stayed at George School until the end of the term but he did not want to go back for the next term as he felt that they had been very unfair to Roger, there could have been an "on campus" punishment. Roger himself meanwhile had been interviewed and accepted at the University of Washington for next year so we all settled down for the summer.

During the summer both the boys worked at various jobs quite a bit of fruit picking in nearby orchards. Roger also worked at the local Jack in the Box as a bus boy but of course we changed the name to Jacques dans la boite, far more upper class!

The boys started their new schools in the fall and things went pretty well to start with! Roger did well in his classes but was not happy with the curriculum, he felt he could learn more from a good book than listening to one of the professors. Perhaps the teaching style was very different from George School though Doug had no problems at the high school level.

As time went on Roger was skipping more classes and finally announced that he was going to hitchhike to some other towns and try other colleges. It amazed me but he did actually sit in on various classes while camping out in various parking lots. Of course he was getting no credits and just doing odd jobs to pay for the necessities - food for example!

Doug graduated from high school and chose the State college in Bellingham rather than the University of Washington, to some extent I think due to Roger's experience. He found lodging in Bellingham and went back and forth on weekends, usually on a motor bike that scared me to death!

On the other side of the family Jake and I carried on day by day. I was doing pretty well in my job, I had had various promotions and as the salary was improving I had paid off all the original loans. Jake could handle minor things like small grocery shopping - but a cook he never would be! We were not happy about Roger of course, we felt he was wasting his talents. Actually part of this was due to his Dad's illness, he knew Jake had studied for years for his CPA degree, giving up on other pleasures to spend time studying then within months of success his brain no longer functioned as it should. And to Roger this meant have fun now, worry later. We could understand his feeling though of course we tried to convince him that his life could be quite different from his Dad's.

Rancho Bernardo, California, 1973

We had many friends but most of our contacts were just by telephone, they all were involved in family events and Jake's handicaps made getting together too difficult. The boys too tended towards out of the house activities, our home was pretty dull. Jake and I too were having a rather distant relationship, I was working long hours and I was tired and probably not as close as I should have been. We had for example split into two different bedrooms due to sleeping difficulties. The only way Jake could move in bed was by pulling himself over on a rope and swing setup over the bed and when he did this it always woke me up. He did the rollover barely awake but I was awake for hours afterwards and off to work very short on sleep. So after many months we decided to use separate bedrooms and it did help me to get more sleep and get to work with my brain working.

In spite of everything it came as an incredible shock when at the end of dinner one evening with the boys Jake announced that he had that day seen an attorney and was divorcing me. I was absolutely stunned, dead silence at the table then Roger got up, said to Doug, "Lets go" and the two of them left. My immediate reaction was one of guilt, what had I done - or not done to create Jake's desire to separate.

I asked Jake about getting together and starting over but he absolutely refused to consider it. I spoke to a few close friends they were all stunned at the mere thought of it but also all told me to see an attorney. The boys did not want to talk about it, I had no help from them. I think they just did not want to feel as if they would be taking sides. So I finally did face up to things and went to see an attorney.

Meanwhile a strange thing occurred. I had not told anybody at work about the divorce possibility and the very day that I made the appointment with the attorney the Regional Vice President called me into his office and told me that I had been promoted and they wanted to transfer me to San Diego where a new company complex in a place called Rancho Bernardo was under construction. Half of me did not want to leave my home or move from the boys but the other half felt that it would be a good start, new area, new friends.

I had a week to make my decision and I decided to go to San Diego. I flew down with the boss for a few days to see the area and the partially built office building. The next month was hectic, sometimes rather miserable but at least so many things to occupy my mind. From the divorce settlement I received the house while Jake got our land at Northgate (in Seattle) and all savings accounts. As I would be leaving town I immediately put the house on the market. It was not a good time, Seattle thrived on Boeings and they were on strike and houses were practically being given away.

Doug was still in Western Washington college in Bellingham living in a small apartment there and Roger was still working whatever jobs could be found, also living in Bellingham. Jake rented a small apartment that he thought he could manage and the boys helped him move furniture etc.

We also had to decide what to do about our dog Foxie. I could not take her to San Diego. Johnny, our friend and a vet

Rancho Bernardo, California, 1973

said if the boys took her he would take care of anything that came up with no charge for anything. That was nice. Actually there was a rather sad ending to the Foxie story. The boys came down to Seattle to help at my garage sale and when they went back to Bellingham Foxie had disappeared. And this is where Roger brought me to what he had previously said that if Foxie ran away she would be unhappy because she thought we didn't love her. Oh dear, what "pets" will do.

A good thing happened when a friend who had a relation living near San Diego asked if she could go with me then we could share the driving and have company all the way. It sounded like a good idea to me and so after all the last minute things to do, the furniture was moved and I was on my way. The house was still on the market; not too many people interested.

The trip down to San Diego went well. I dropped my friend off at a bus station where she could get a brief ride to her cousin and then I went into the city and got myself a motel room. From then on life was interesting to say the least. I found my way to the temporary office rooms and the site where the new office would be, construction being in the last stages. I also had to take care of food for myself, fixing a few things but mostly eating out.

A few people being transferred here from other Regional Offices I met as we worked in the temporary office but most of them were married men who were gone on the weekends as they went back to their families. Of course the big thing for me was to look for a house to buy. I wanted to get one close to the new office as at that time gas was in a semi-rationing programme, based on your car's license number you could only get gas on certain days of the week. We had no idea how long that would go on so it made sense to live near the office as it was in a residential neighbourhood .

I took the plunge with a small two bedroom house chosen largely because it had a large yard with a beautiful green lawn that I would hate later (too much upkeep!). It was just a few blocks from the office so convenient in that way.

I made friends with my new working companions and my boss, the Underwriting Manager, was my former boss from Seattle and we got along well making it easy with so many things to adjust to.

So time went on and my life got into an ordinary routine; friends made at work and friends made in the neighbourhood. I was financially not wealthy but able to live comfortably with help from a recent promotion. I had hoped that the boys would consider moving down but neither of them were interested in California, both having recently found jobs they liked in Seattle.

Epilogue

Audrey, my mother, lived in Rancho Bernardo from 1973 until 2002. She continued working for Allstate Insurance, achieving the highest position a woman had held in the company, until she retired in 1985.

She had a large cactus garden which kept her busy and had a number of friends in her immediate neighborhood, mostly on the same cul de sac street. I think she was happy after a lifetime of England and Seattle to be in a mild sunny climate.

She was an avid walker throughout her years in Rancho Bernardo and even played golf now and again.

She also, for quite a few years after retiring, took trips once or twice a year to many destinations around the world with travel groups. Truly, to every corner of the earth.

I moved to Northern California in 1980 and was able to visit her on a fairly regular basis. Doug continued living in Washington state but was able to make it down to Rancho Bernardo now and again, and occasionally we'd visited her together.

In 2002, she moved to a classy home for the elderly near Pasadena, where she lived until she passed away in March of 2013 at the age of 92.

About the Author

Audrey, known to me simply as Mom was a good mother. Now I know everybody is supposed to say that but she really was. She, like my father, was an honest high integrity person.

She worked hard, being the bread winner, and provided for the family but beyond that she enjoyed giving. She liked to cook and made us jam and cookies and I think she even liked it when we stole cookies out of the freezer that we weren't supposed to touch. She loved the family experience of Christmas and any family events. We had several foster children over the years and it meant a lot to her to help those who had less than us.

She enjoyed playing Cribbage and Bezique.

She read a lot, often knitting while she read. Or she would knit while watching TV. She liked British television series, whodunits and loved Perry Mason.

She has also written some children's poems.

- Roger

Photos

Audrey in an English Garden

Mum

Dad

Audrey and Jake Just Married

Young Couple in Washington

The Family at the LFP Construction Site

The author about the time she wrote her memoirs

Books by Roger Brown

The Truth Seeker's Handbook has been published in print and as an eBook. I kept journals for over 20 years, writing almost every day. Much of the philosophy, the struggles leading to learning and the attitudes that helped me get through life appears in this book. It has a section dealing with major life themes, one about our relationship to the Earth, one retelling stories of serendipity, and finally a section of reminders to help along the way. Reminders is one of the 4 sections that make up Truth Seeker's Handbook.

Excerpt from The Truth Seeker's Handbook:

> Delight in truth at all costs. We really must accept everything we experience. Simply say, yes, this is happening to me. We tend to avoid and repress and choose against less pleasant feelings. What a rip-off! They offer powerful information as to what is going on; information as to the reason why we don't at the moment have pleasant feelings. The desirable feelings validate flow and rightness. The unpleasant ones are the ones needing the most attention.

- - -

Insights has been published in print and as an eBook. This is a compilation of most of the journal entries which didn't appear in any of my other books, but that I felt needed to see the light of day. I organized them into such categories as Cosmic, Philosophy and Attitude, Love, Society, and several more.

Excerpt from Insights:

I heard Earth Angel on the radio today and thought about the American Dream and its surfacing in the 50's and the dreamy songs reflecting it. I was overwhelmed with a rush of rightness. Sure it is distorted. Sure its means are destructive. But the dream - to have comfort and ease and the time and space to relax and expand, time to create, to have comfortable homes is fine. It sparked a spiritual movement which unfortunately was complicated by an awesome opportunity to be corrupted by material and sensory numbing diversions. But the dream itself, it's not only the American Dream but a soul's dream. To mellow a life in a body. To find harmony. I'm all for it.

- - -

Heading Out is poetry and prose and has been published in print and as an eBook. Cryptic and cosmic might be good words to describe these writings; word adventures. Poetry is an individual thing and I can't say for sure you will like them, but look for it and check out the free eBook sample.

A short poem from Heading Out:

> Popsicle process brings freedom ... in heat.
> What was ice yields a watery treat.
> When we allow ourselves to have what we need
> That water fertilizes and brings life to our seed.

Encounters has been published in print and as an eBook. It is about encounters with women in my life that were romantic and sometimes intimate but does not include the girlfriends or lovers of duration. It is all journal entries in real time; usually my initial feelings, the encounter evolving, and finally myself seeking resolution and completion for myself and hopefully us. These encounters took place mostly during my 20's and 30's and are very gutsy and emotional. I have been a very emotional person and it may surprise some people to read a man's feelings essentially unedited.

Excerpt from Encounters:

> I approached her during a thunderstorm downpour on the main sunning deck (at Harbin Hot Springs). I was attracted to her and felt an immediate thrill from and affection for her. I wanted her. I spent some time with her and got to know her a little. I slept next to her on the sleeping deck. She let me know she needed space. She removed my hand gently from her body, but didn't let go. She held my hand a few moments more. What a beautiful softening of the space between us that she required. I was hurt and felt rejected, although I appreciated her communication and integrity. I cried. Strange sleep. Dreams. I felt again defeated but fought it, hung in there.

- - -

33 Years of Dreams has been published in print and as an eBook. Over a period of 33 years I wrote down a ton of dreams. A friend once said to me, why would anybody want to read anyone else's dreams? That got me to thinking but it came to me you could also ask why would anybody want to read anyone else's poetry? They are the same, in a way; kind of cryptic non-linear stories that take images and create something to be interpreted. After trimming out some of the uninteresting and poorly transcribed dreams it is, in its final form, almost 700 pages and is published in 2 volumes. They are for sale individually.

A dream from 33 Years of Dreams:

> I was with a pet, female, smiling Buffalo and a group of friends hanging out in the country. And with an alien friend who materialized to be with us. There was a river scene, after going through a gate. Rednecks were hassling us, then we saw three of our women being physically abused down the road a ways, by three men. We headed down in force (with our alien and Buffalo) to deal with it.

Where to Buy the Books

To buy the books in print go to my Author Page:
http://books2read.com/rogergoldenbrown

Versions of these books in eBook format can all be found at Smashwords, as well as free sample downloads:
https://www.smashwords.com/profile/view/Rogue17

Check out my Smashwords author interview here:
https://www.smashwords.com/profile/view/Rogue17154

www.ingramcontent.com/pod-product-compliance
Lightning Source LLC
LaVergne TN
LVHW041620070426
835507LV00008B/367